BEST-LOVED
QUILT PATTERNS

Copyright 1987 by Oxmoor House, Inc.
Book Division of Southern Progress Corporation
P.O. Box 2463, Birmingham, Alabama 35201

Library of Congress Catalog Card Number: 87-050324
ISBN: 0-8487-0723-0
Manufactured in the United States of America
Second Printing 1988

Executive Editor: Candace N. Conard
Production Manager: Jerry Higdon
Associate Production Manager: Rick Litton
Art Director: Bob Nance

Best-Loved Quilt Patterns

Editor: Carol Cook Hagood
Editorial Assistant: Josie E. Lee
Photographer: Gary Clark
Artist: Larry Hunter
Mechanical Artist: Jane Bonds
Designer: Cindy Cooper

BEST-LOVED
QUILT PATTERNS

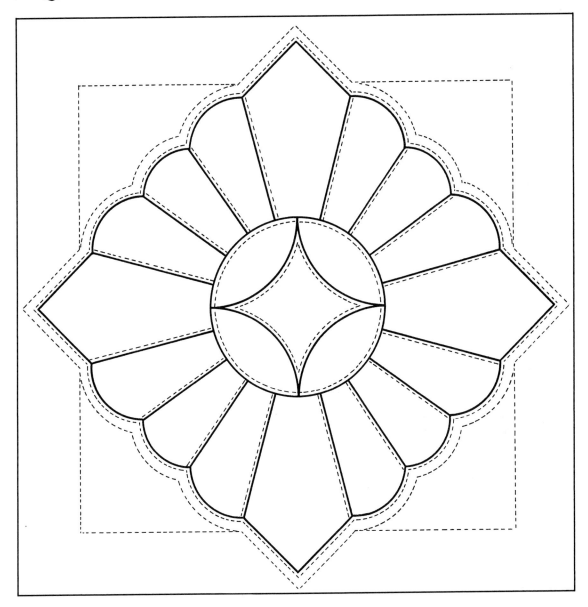

Oxmoor
House®

Contents

continued . . .

Contents, continued

Introduction

Finding full-sized patterns for your patchwork projects can be time-consuming. There you are, with an irresistible array of fabrics to piece and appliqué. But before you can even begin to work, you may check dozens of quilt books looking for ideas, then spend hours more drafting or enlarging designs. No more! In this treasury of 50 best-loved quilt blocks, you'll find the full-sized patterns you need, ready to trace and enjoy.

How did we decide which patterns to include? Quilting friends from around the country suggested patterns for this special collection. You're sure to find many of your favorites among the selections, which include Fancy Dresden Plate, Carolina Lily, Flying Geese, Star of Bethlehem, Whig Rose, and many other quilting classics. We've included blocks for piecing, for appliqué, and for combinations of the two techniques. Whether you're a beginning, intermediate, or advanced quilter, you'll find designs to suit your skills and interests.

In the illustrated contents pages, drawings of each quilt block help you quickly identify the traditional patterns you love. For each, there is a full set of patterns, with seam allowance and grain lines clearly marked. A diagram of each block shows the play of lights and darks, suggesting ways you can use light, medium, and dark tones of your favorite colors to bring each square to life.

Make your templates from clear quilter's vinyl or cardboard. Place a sheet of quilter's vinyl (available at craft and needlework stores) directly over the page of the book on which your pattern is found. Trace the pattern onto the vinyl with an indelible pen. Mark the outside cutting edge, the seam allowance, the corner turns (indicated with larger dots) and the grain line for each piece. Label each template with pattern name and total number of pieces to be cut for each block. Cut out each template along solid cutting line. Punch out the corner turns with a very small, ⅛-inch hole punch.

If you prefer to make cardboard templates, trace pattern onto tracing paper and use carbon paper to transfer the design to posterboard or similar-weight cardboard. Label cardboard templates, cut out, and punch out corner turns. If you are using cardboard templates, you'll probably need to make several sets, as the cardboard edge wears down with use and becomes inaccurate.

Wash, dry, and press your fabrics. Place each template on the right side of the fabric, aligning the grain line of template with that of the fabric. If the fabric is printed, position the template to make the best use of any figure, stripe, or other fabric design. Trace around the shape with a pencil or water-erasable pen. Cut out fabric shape; on the wrong side, indicate corner turns by marking through the punched holes in the template.

Now you are ready to assemble the pieces and to build, block by block, whatever size and style quilt you desire. Will it be a graceful President's Wreath or a dramatic Storm at Sea? The colorful mosaic of Grandmother's Flower Garden done up in tiny prints, or the bold geometrics of a red and white Shoo Fly? With the patterns in this book, you can make a series of show-stopping quilts. Or, if you choose, combine a number of block patterns in an inviting sampler quilt design.

Don't overlook the possibilities of sharing the fun. On the next occasion when a group gift is in order, invite your friends to stitch their favorite squares and join them in an old-fashioned friendship quilt.

Explore. Enjoy. However you choose to use these much-loved, traditional patterns, you'll find inspiration here for many hours of delightful quilting.

Birds in the Air

10″ square block; intermediate
2 templates; 40 pieces

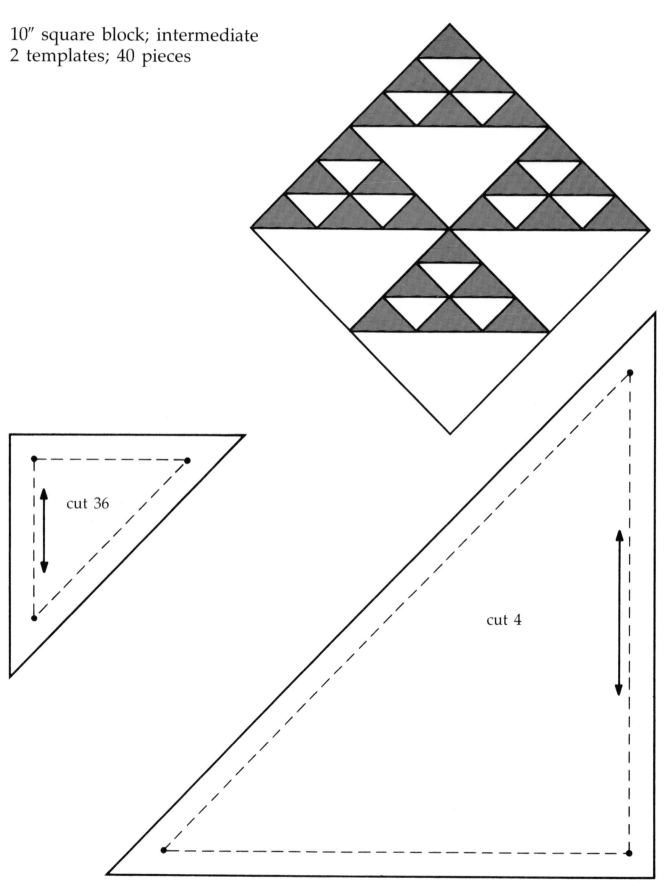

cut 36

cut 4

Bear's Paw

10″ square block; intermediate
4 templates; 49 pieces

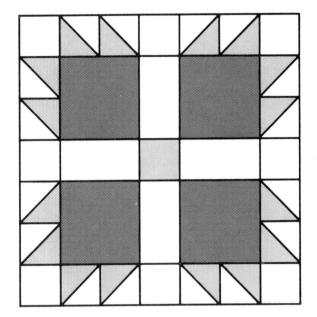

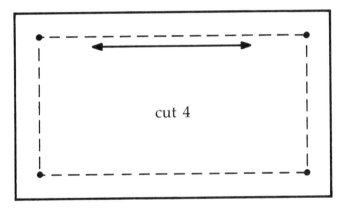
cut 4

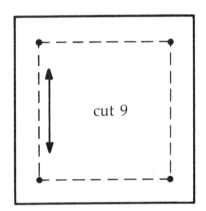
cut 9

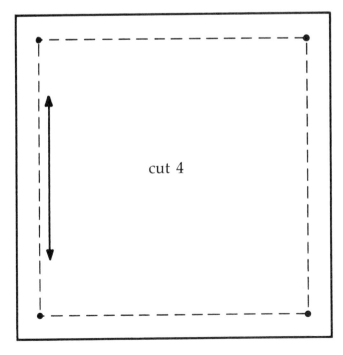
cut 4

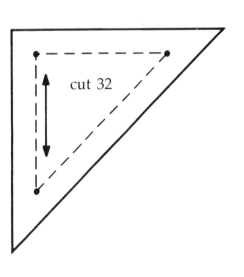
cut 32

11

Shoo Fly

10″ square block; beginner
3 templates; 13 pieces

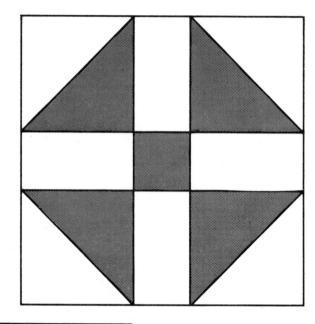

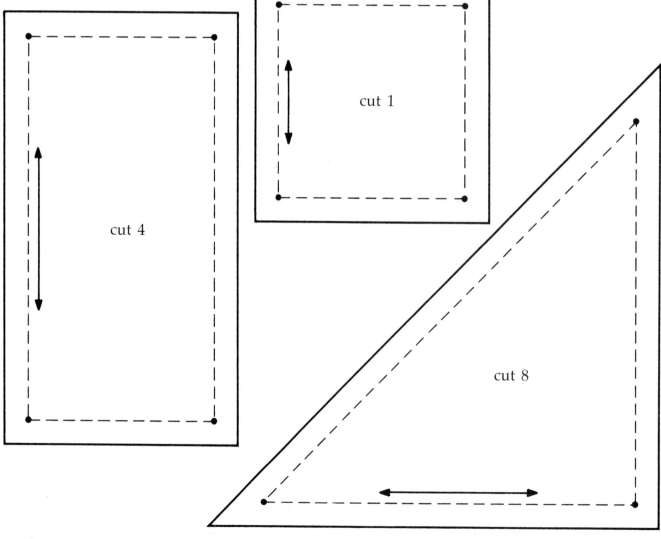

cut 4

cut 1

cut 8

Anvil

10″ square block; beginner
3 templates; 16 pieces

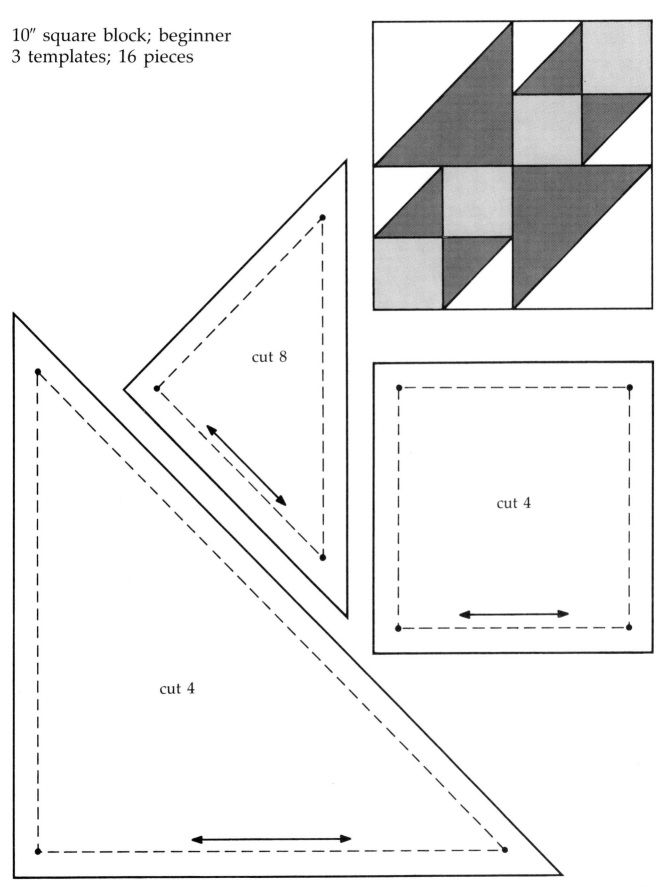

cut 8

cut 4

cut 4

Baskets

10″ square block; intermediate
4 templates; 40 pieces

cut 4

cut 16

cut 12

cut 8

Double Nine Patch

10″ square block; beginner
3 templates; 17 pieces

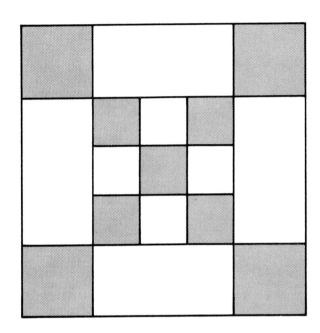

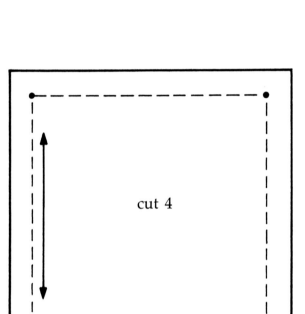

cut 4

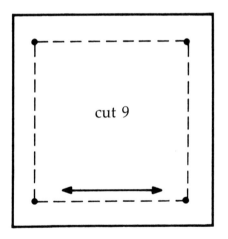

cut 9

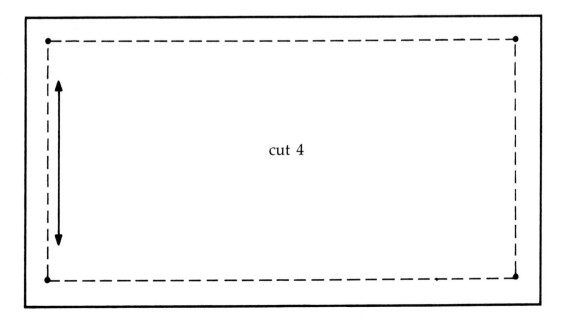

cut 4

Joseph's Necktie

10″ square block; beginner
3 templates; 24 pieces

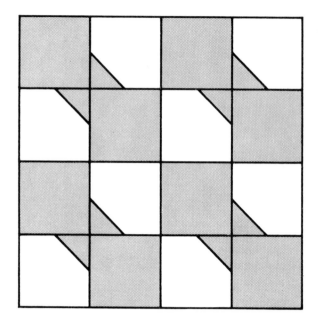

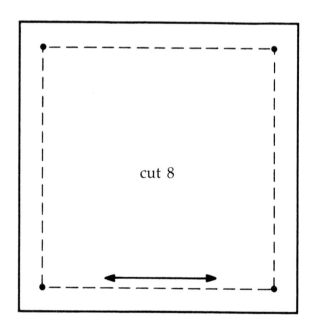

cut 8

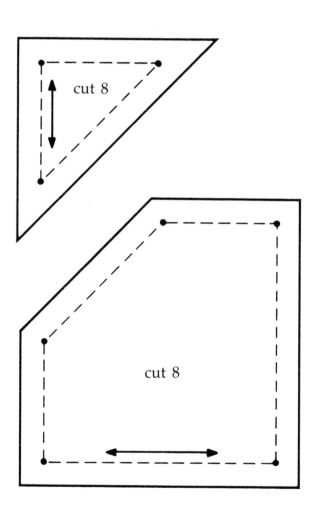

cut 8

cut 8

Spools

10″ square block; intermediate
2 templates; 20 pieces

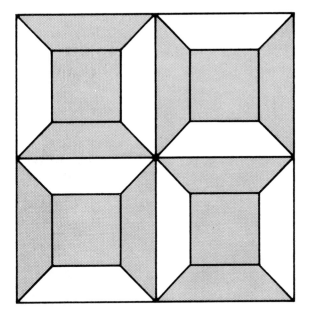

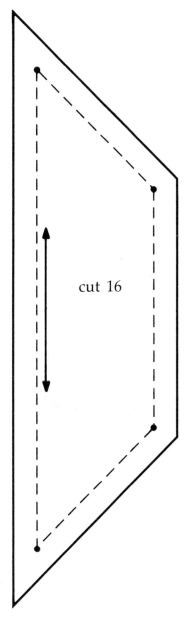

cut 16

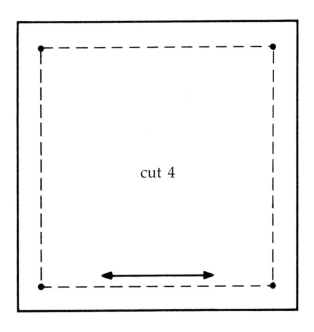

cut 4

Log Cabin

10" square block; beginner
10 templates; 19 pieces

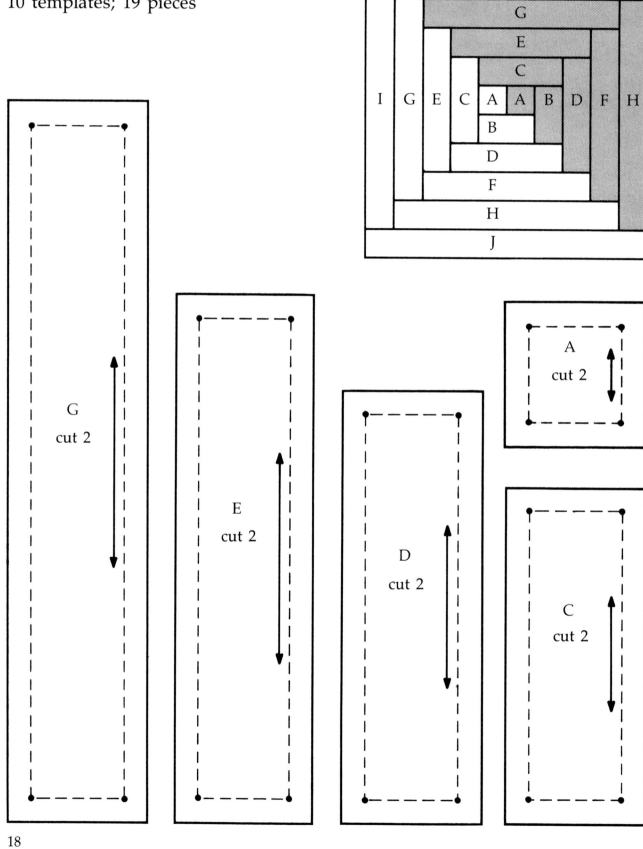

G
cut 2

E
cut 2

D
cut 2

A
cut 2

C
cut 2

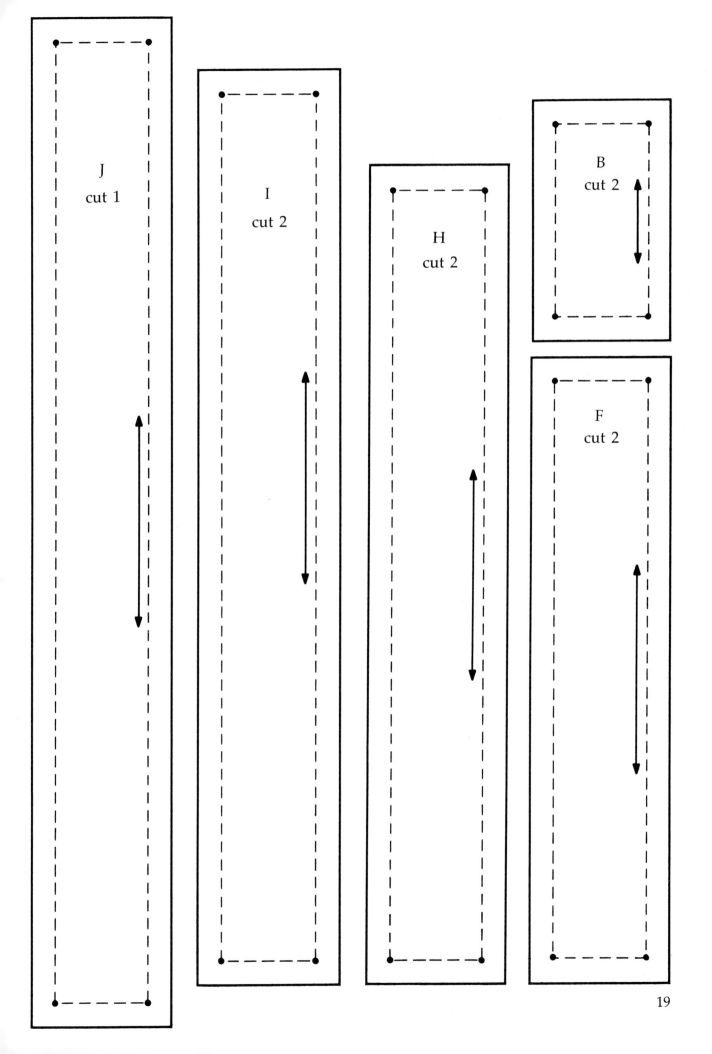

J
cut 1

I
cut 2

H
cut 2

B
cut 2

F
cut 2

House

10″ square block; intermediate
11 templates; 22 pieces

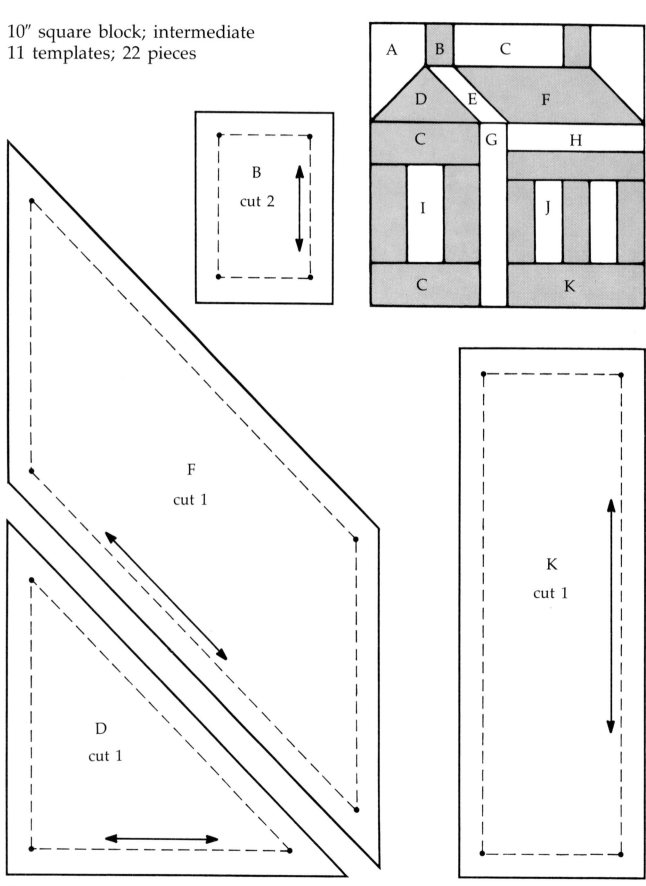

B
cut 2

F
cut 1

D
cut 1

K
cut 1

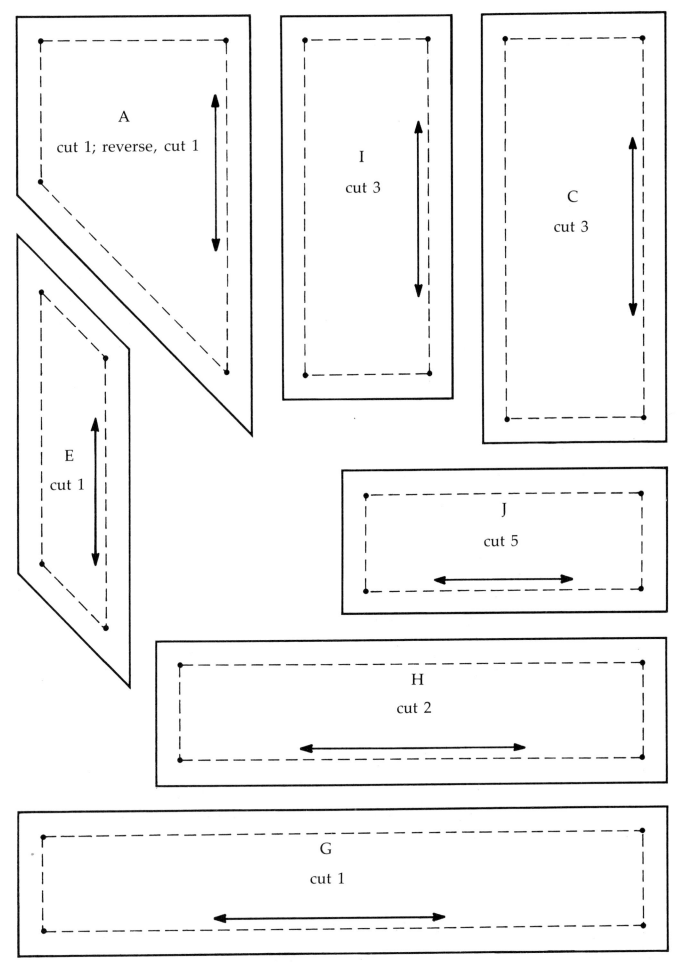

A

cut 1; reverse, cut 1

I

cut 3

C

cut 3

E

cut 1

J

cut 5

H

cut 2

G

cut 1

21

Sailboat

10″ square block; intermediate
4 templates; 17 pieces

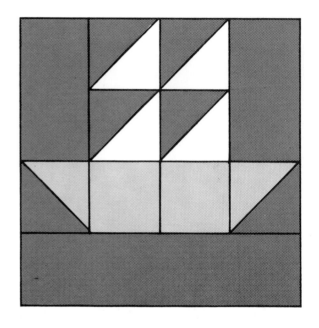

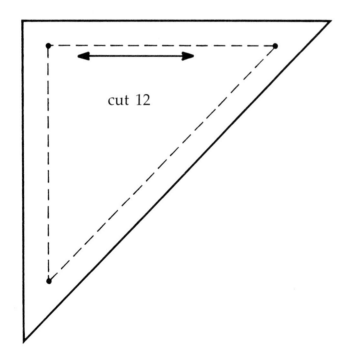

cut 12

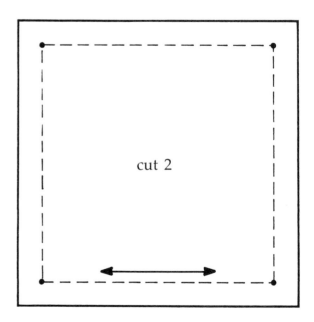

cut 2

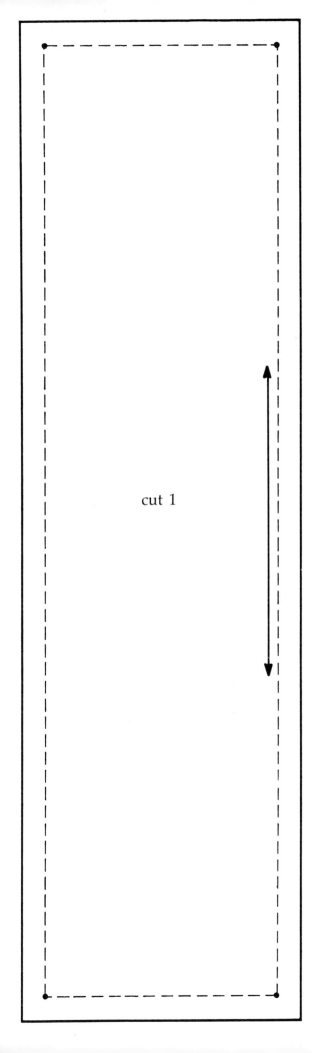

cut 1

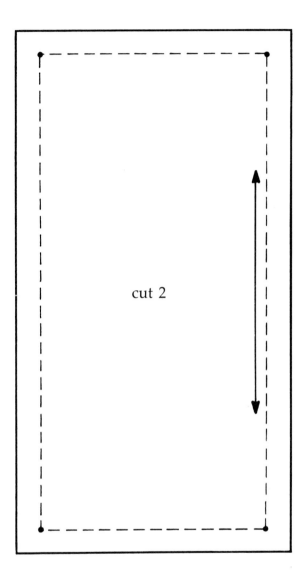

cut 2

Patience Corner

10″ square block; beginner
3 templates; 12 pieces

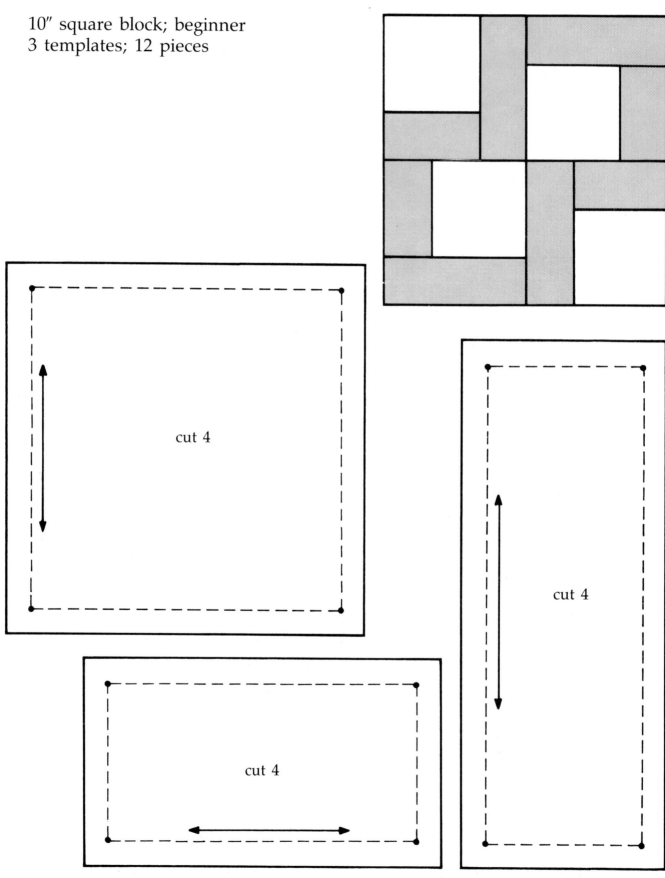

cut 4

cut 4

cut 4

Attic Windows

10″ square block; intermediate
2 templates; 12 pieces

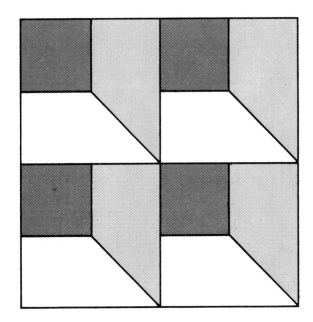

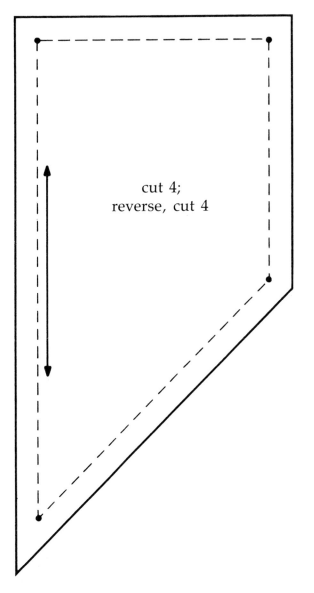

cut 4;
reverse, cut 4

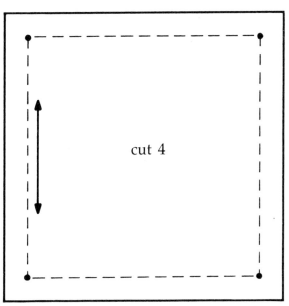

cut 4

Card Tricks

10″ square block; beginner
4 templates; 16 pieces

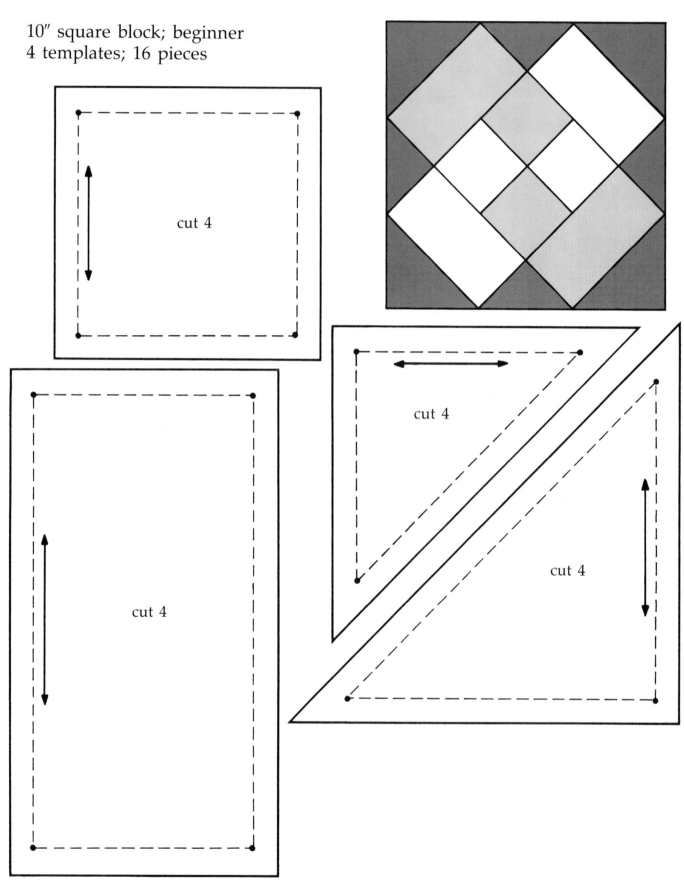

cut 4

cut 4

cut 4

cut 4

Rail Fence

10″ square block; beginner
1 template; 16 pieces

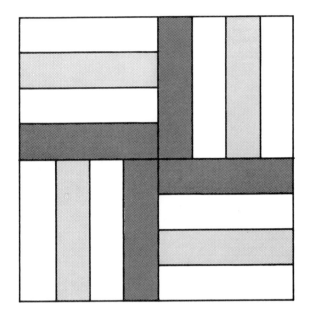

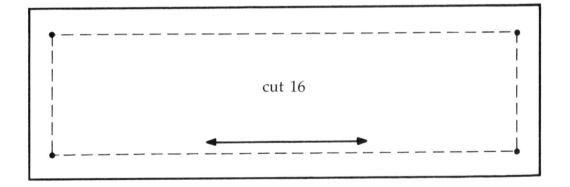

cut 16

Ocean Waves

10" square block; intermediate
2 templates; 26 pieces

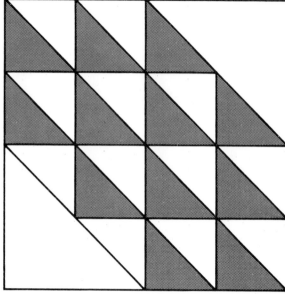

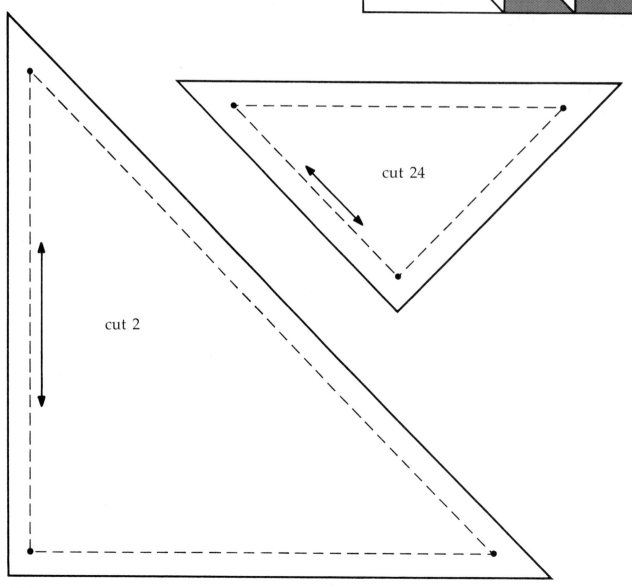

cut 24

cut 2

Cats & Mice

10″ square block; intermediate
3 templates; 29 pieces

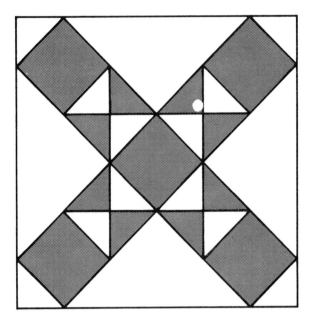

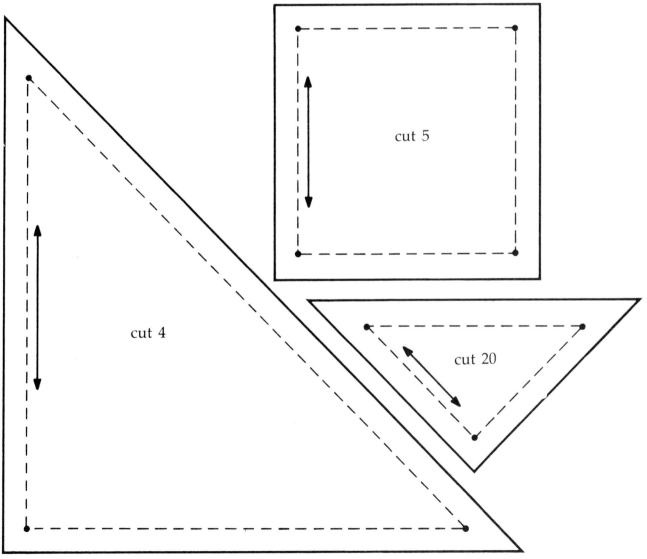

cut 5

cut 4

cut 20

Cake Stand

10″ square block; intermediate
5 templates; 20 pieces

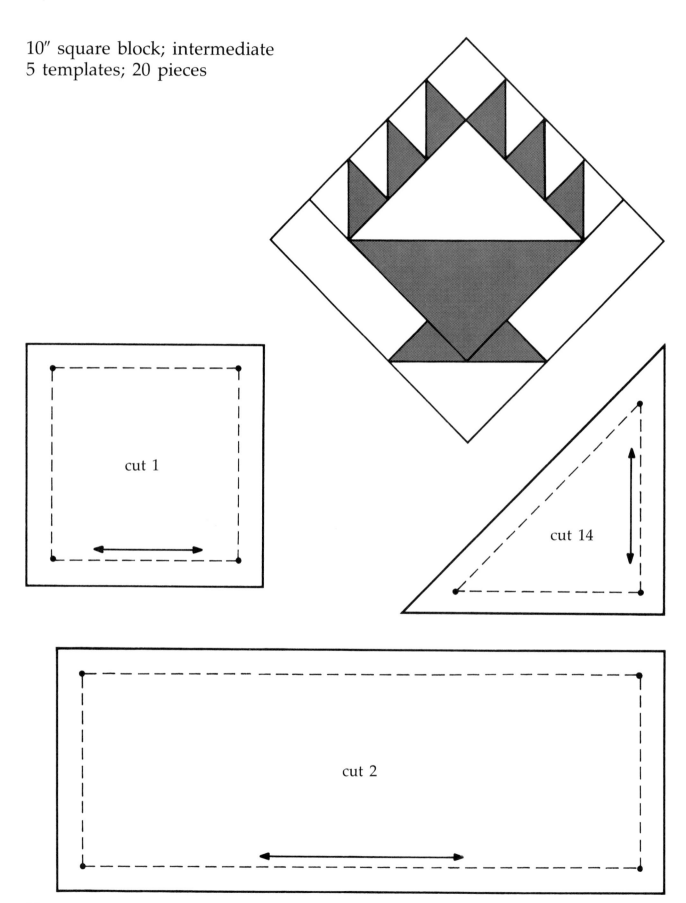

cut 1

cut 14

cut 2

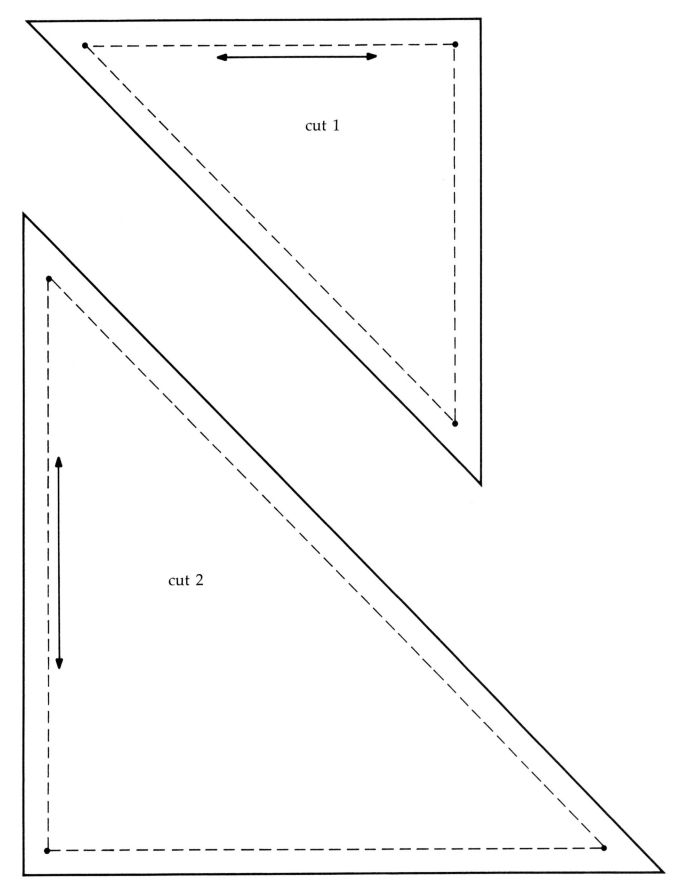

cut 1

cut 2

Diamond in a Square

10″ square block; intermediate
5 templates; 13 pieces

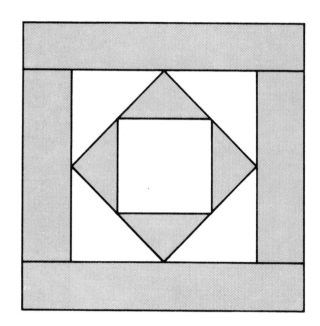

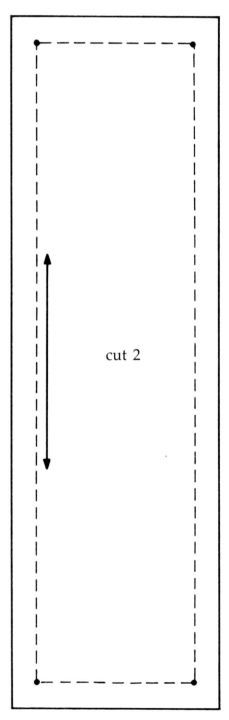

cut 2

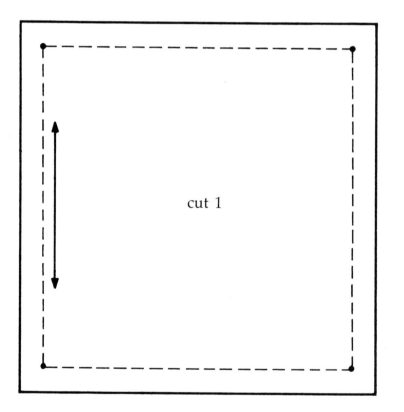

cut 1

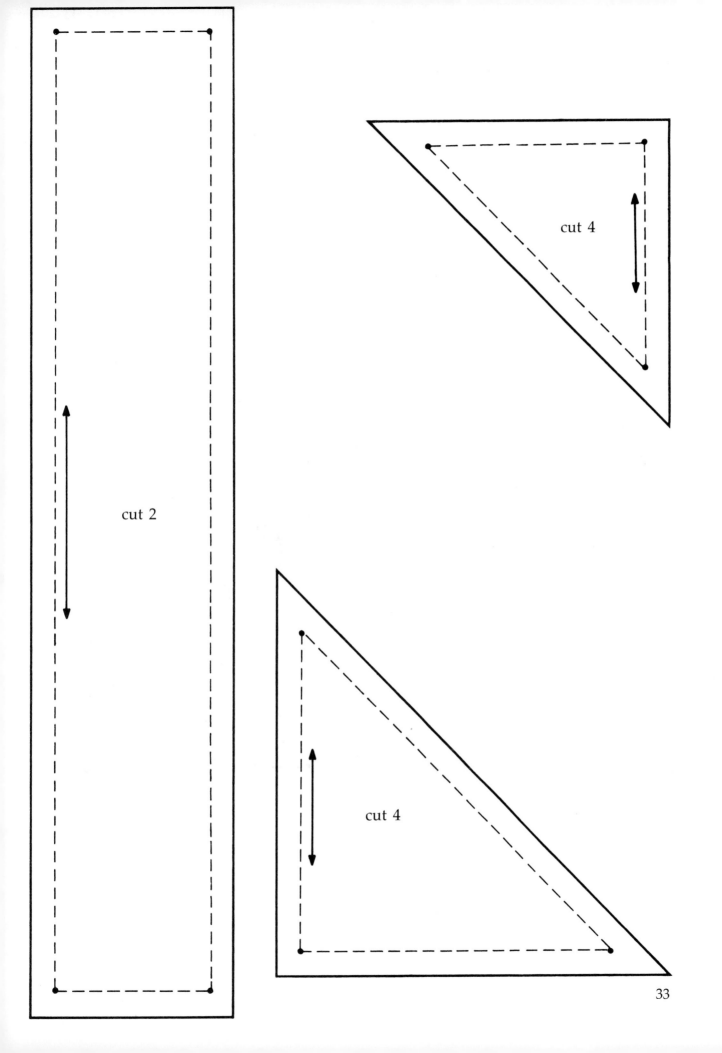

cut 2

cut 4

cut 4

33

Pine Tree

10″ square block; intermediate
5 templates; 42 pieces

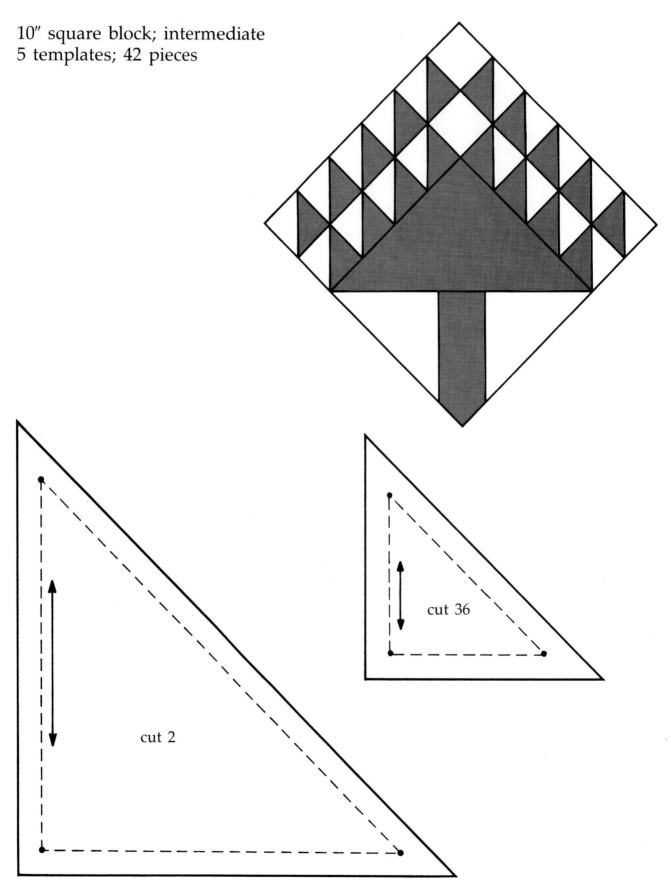

cut 36

cut 2

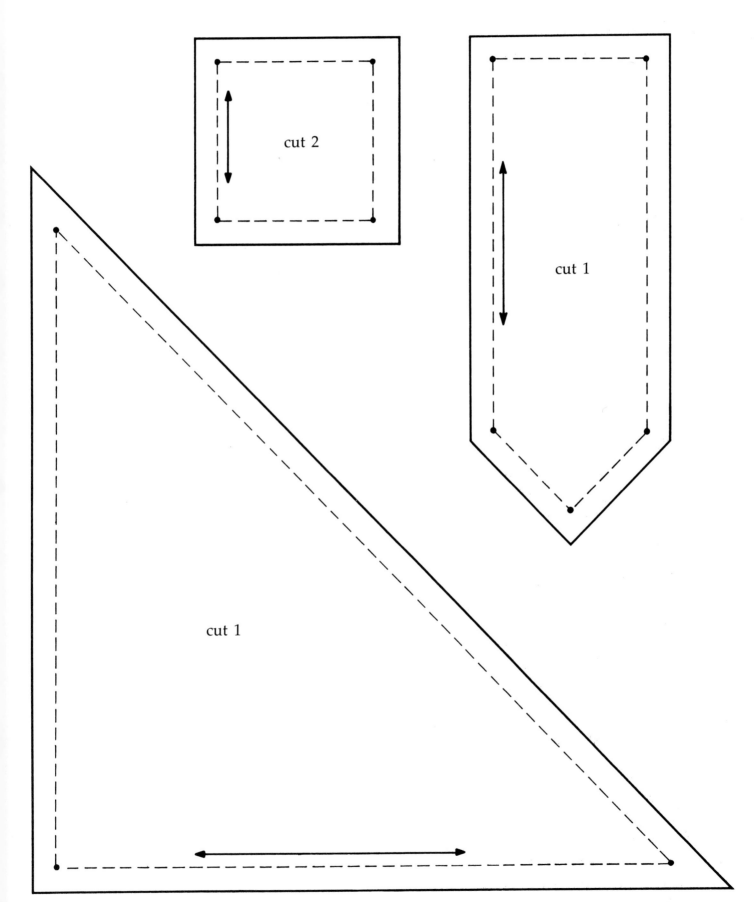

cut 2

cut 1

cut 1

Seven Sisters

Hexagonal block; 9″ on each side;
  advanced
2 templates; 66 pieces

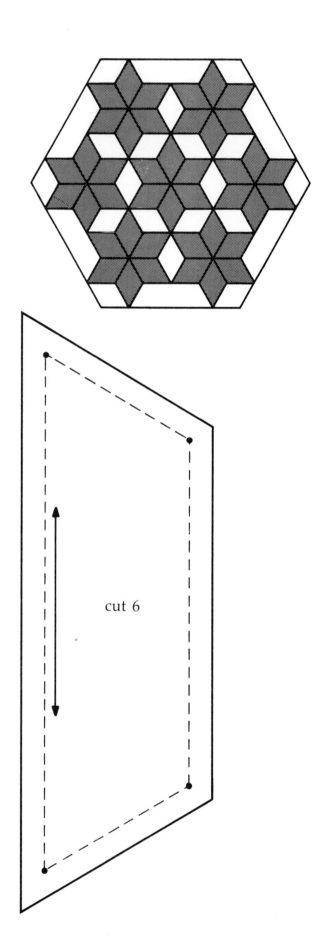

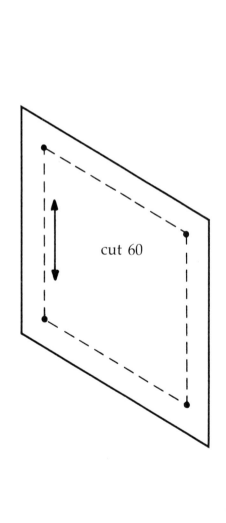

cut 60

cut 6

Grandmother's Flower Garden

Hexagonal block, 10″ on each side;
  intermediate
1 template; 37 pieces

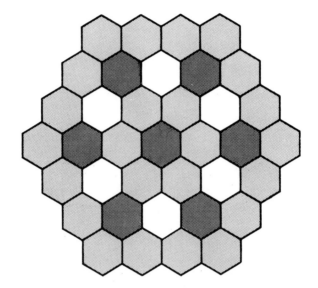

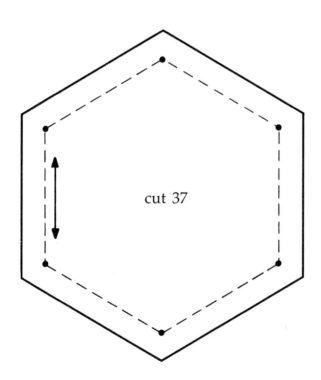

cut 37

Fancy Dresden Plate

10″ square block; intermediate
5 templates; 22 pieces
(including background square)

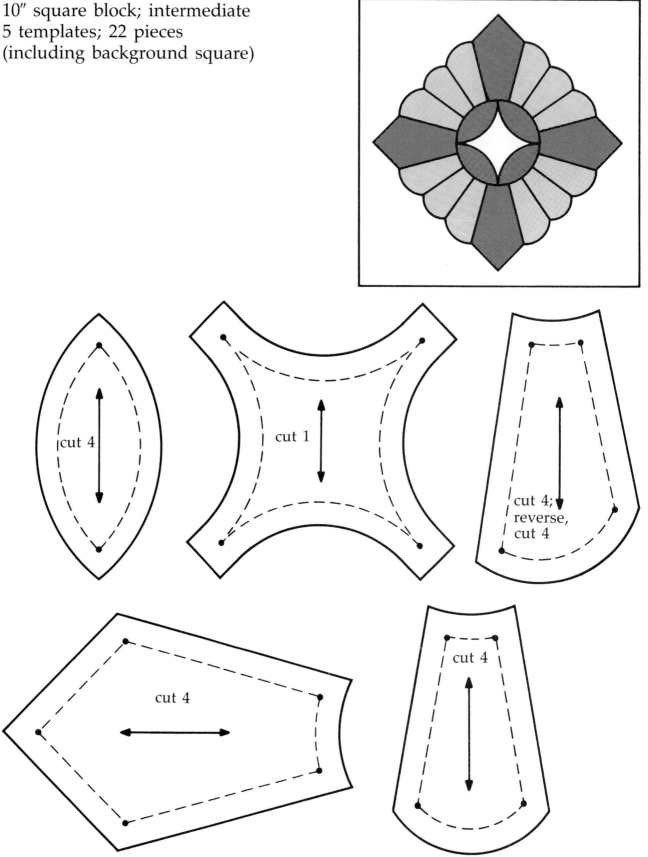

Coffee Cup

10″ square block; intermediate
6 templates; 9 pieces

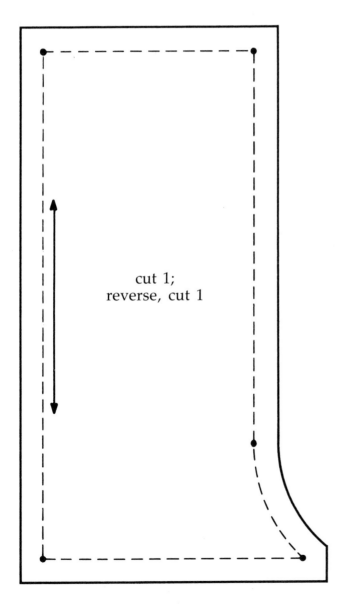

cut 1;
reverse, cut 1

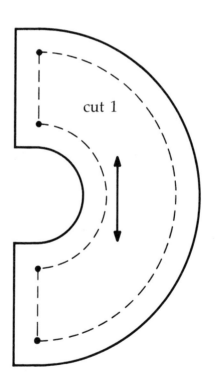

cut 1

continued . . .

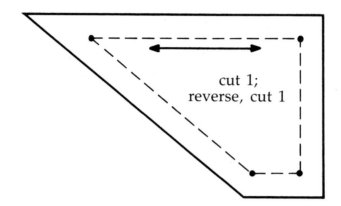

cut 1;
reverse, cut 1

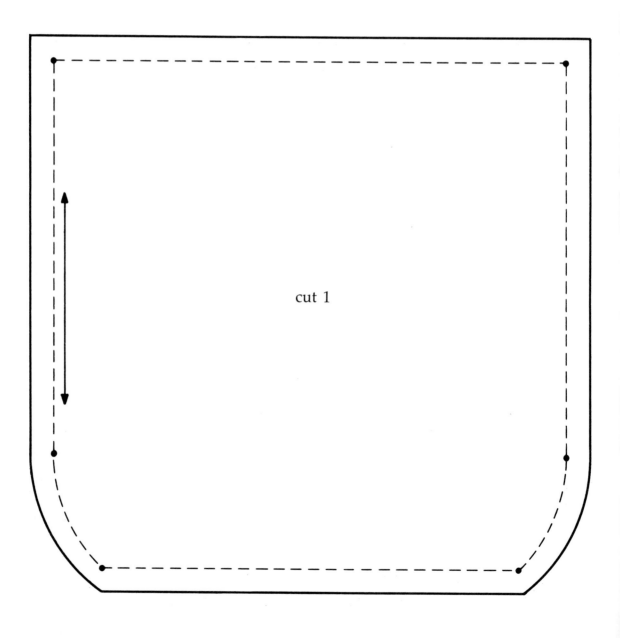

cut 1

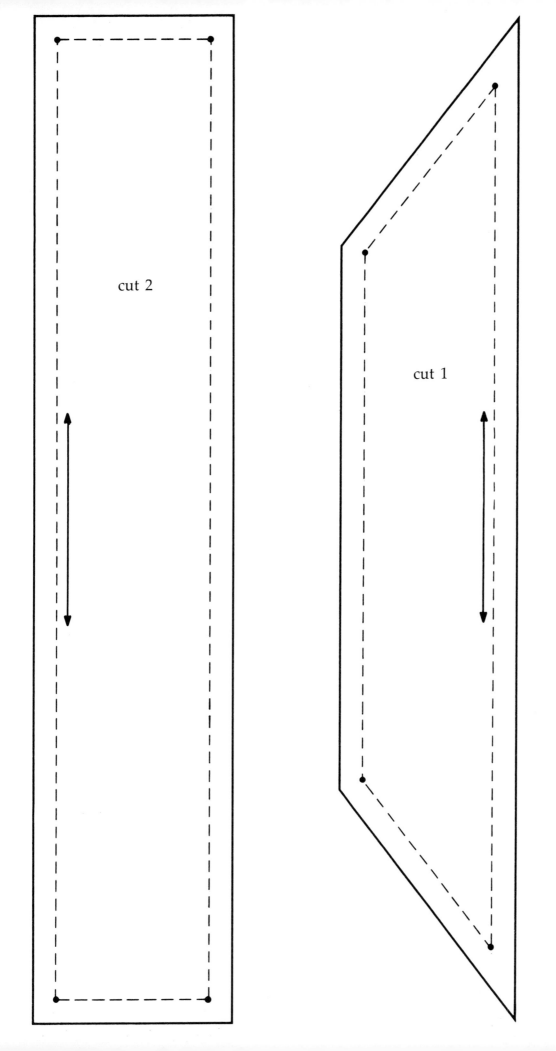

cut 2

cut 1

41

Friendship Knot

10″ square block; intermediate
6 templates; 37 pieces

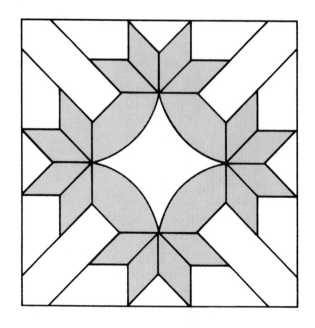

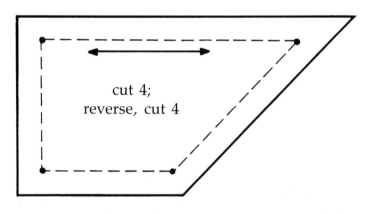

cut 4;
reverse, cut 4

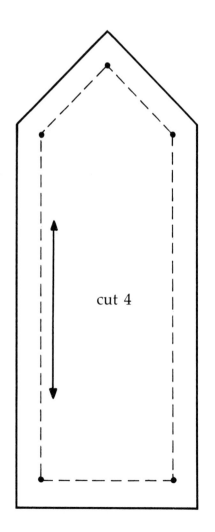

cut 4

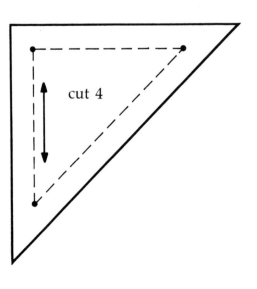

cut 4

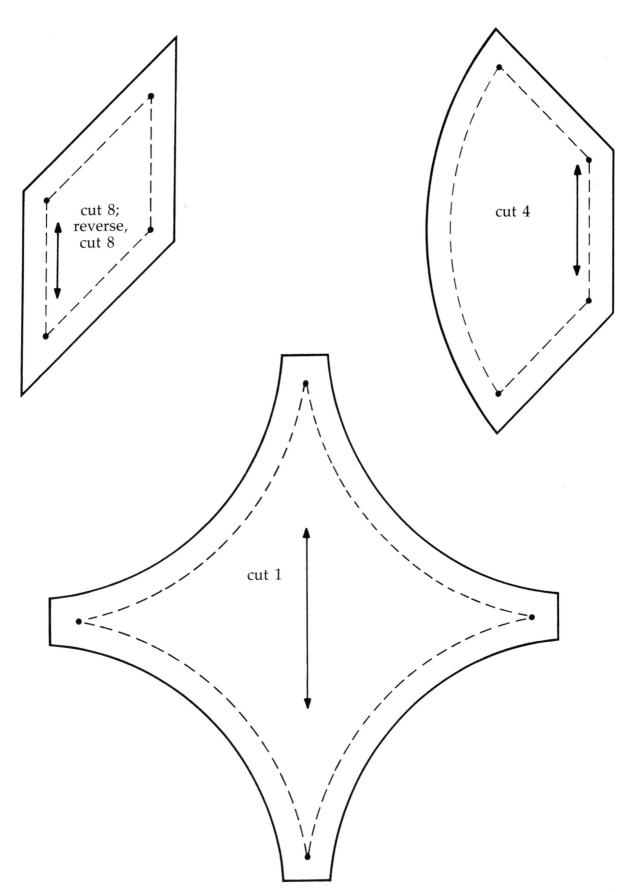

cut 8;
reverse,
cut 8

cut 4

cut 1

Turkey Tracks

10″ square block; intermediate
5 templates; 25 pieces

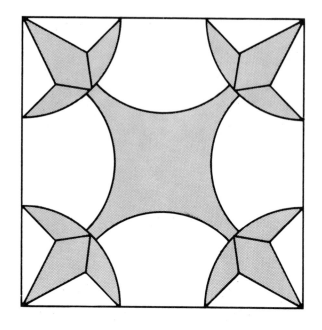

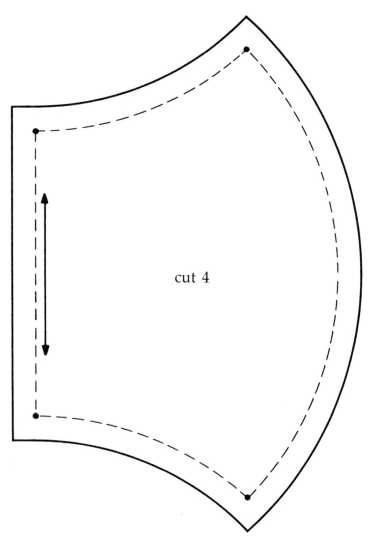

cut 4

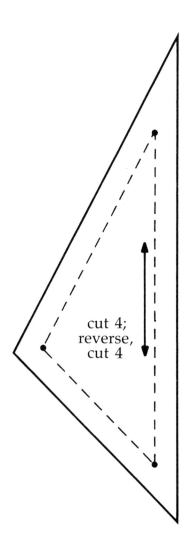

cut 4;
reverse,
cut 4

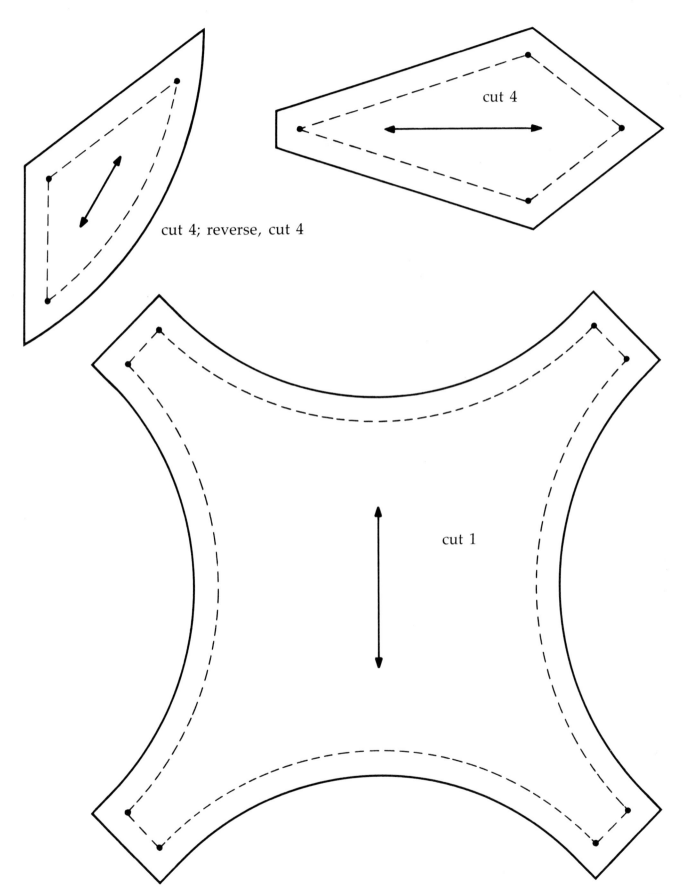

cut 4

cut 4; reverse, cut 4

cut 1

Butterfly

10″ square block; intermediate
7 templates; 13 pieces
(including background square)

Appliqué body after
piecing wings.

Embroider antennae.

cut 1;
reverse, cut 1

cut 1;
reverse, cut 1

cut 1

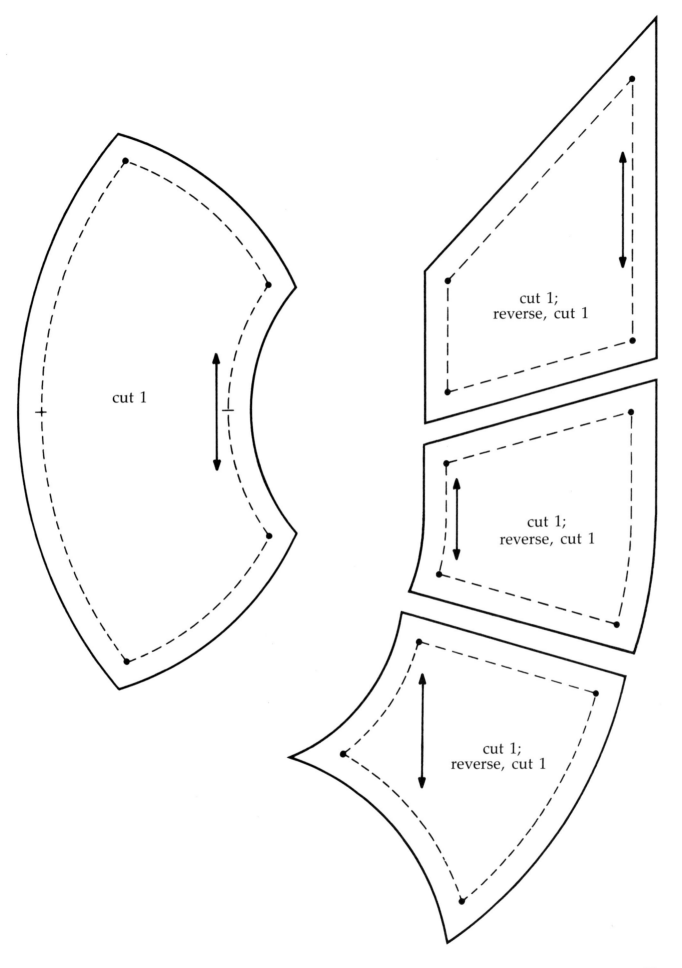

cut 1

cut 1;
reverse, cut 1

cut 1;
reverse, cut 1

cut 1;
reverse, cut 1

47

Double Irish Chain

Two 10″ square blocks—alternate for
   overall pattern; beginner
1 template; 25 pieces for Block A
3 templates; 9 pieces for Block B

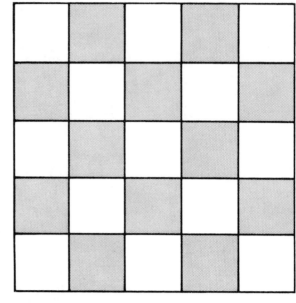

Block A

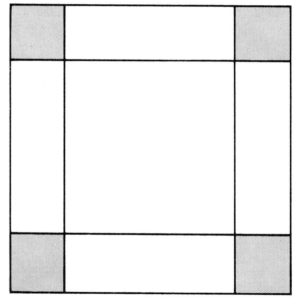

Block B

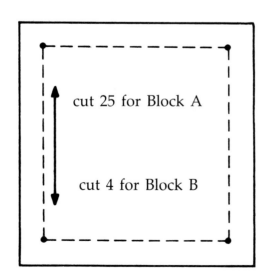

cut 25 for Block A

cut 4 for Block B

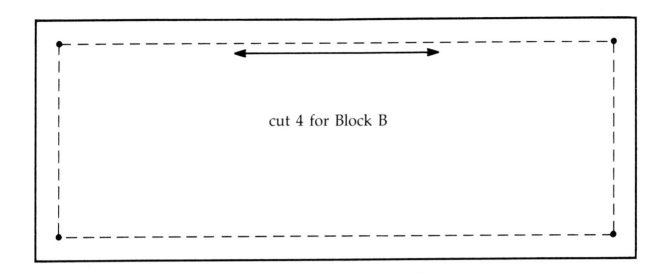

cut 4 for Block B

cut 1 for Block B

Storm at Sea

10″ square block; intermediate
6 templates; 45 pieces

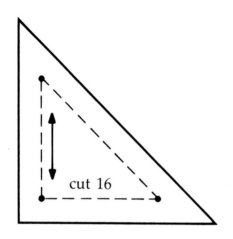

cut 16

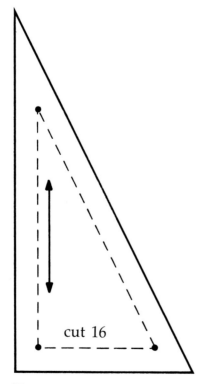

cut 16

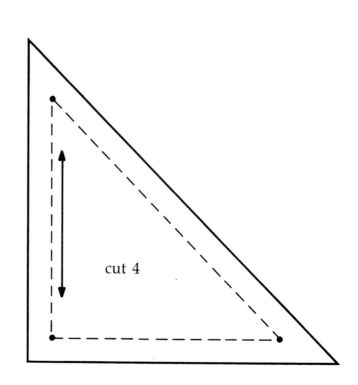

cut 4

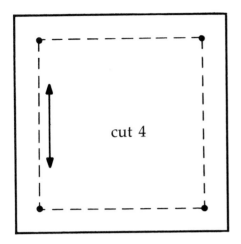

cut 4

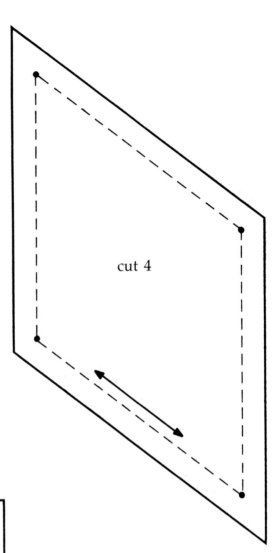

cut 4

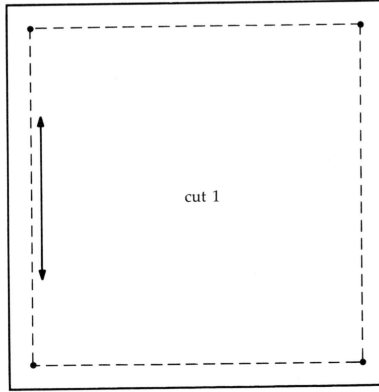

cut 1

Clay's Choice

10″ square block; intermediate
4 templates; 16 pieces

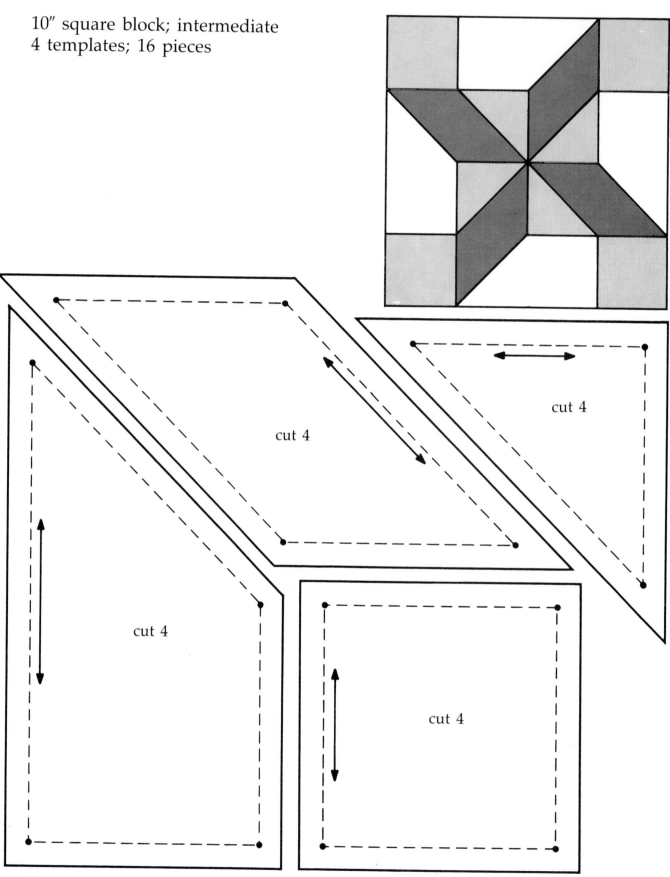

cut 4

cut 4

cut 4

cut 4

Pinwheel

10″ square block; beginner
2 templates; 16 pieces

cut 4

cut 12

Star of Bethlehem

10″ square; advanced
4 templates; 52 pieces

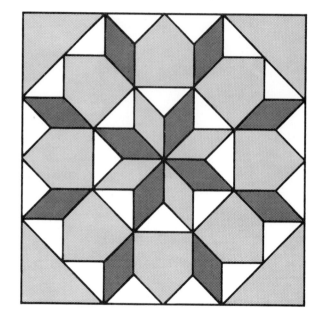

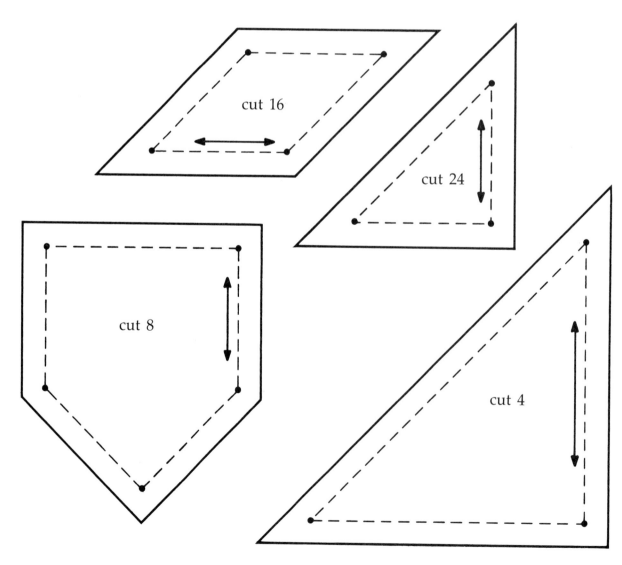

cut 16

cut 24

cut 8

cut 4

Hexagonal Star

Hexagonal block, 10″ on each side;
  beginner
1 template; 12 pieces

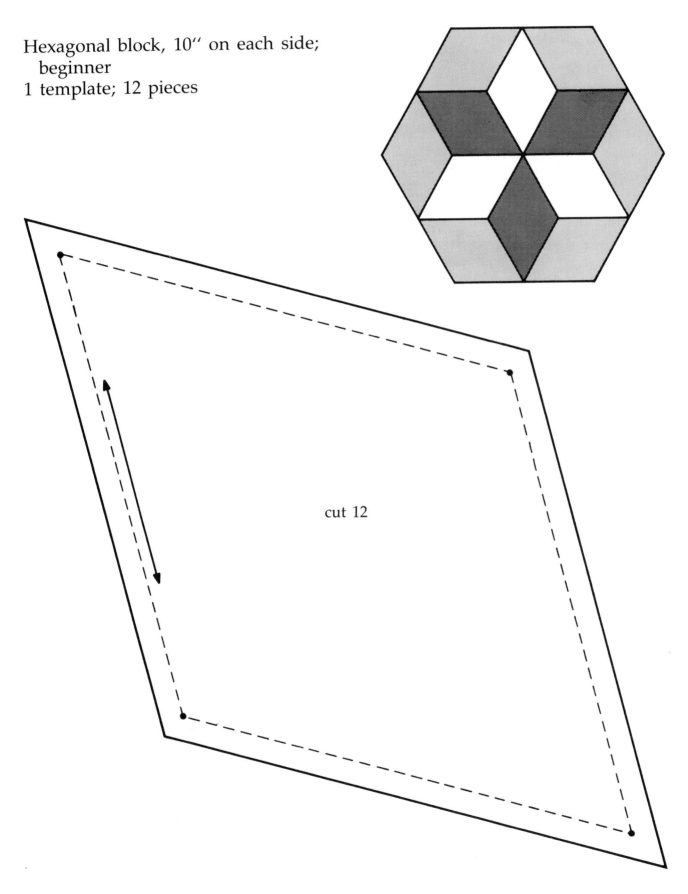

cut 12

Lemoyne Star

10" square block; intermediate
3 templates; 24 pieces

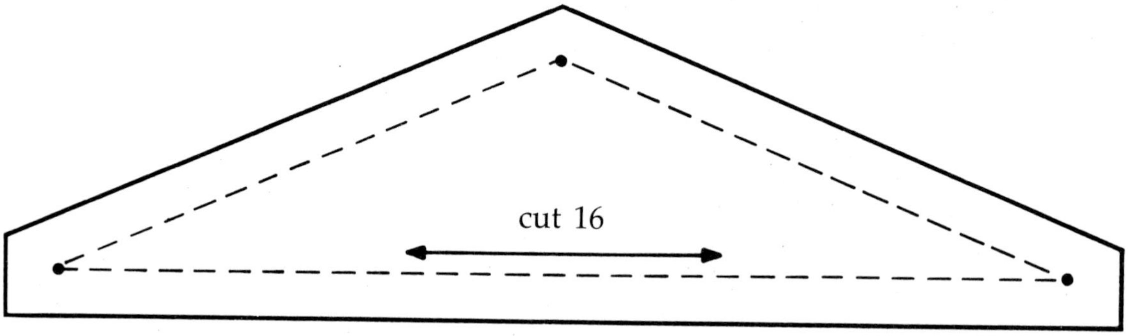

cut 16

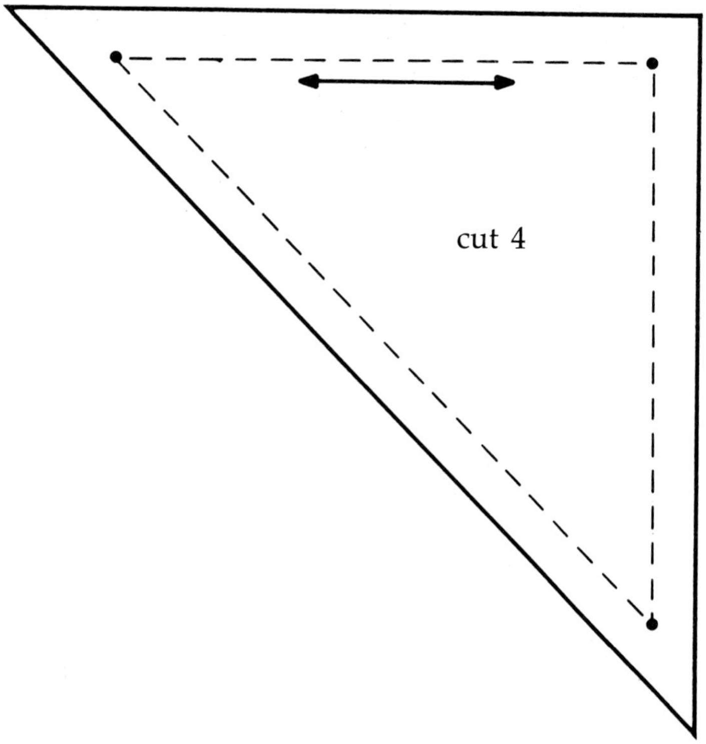

cut 4

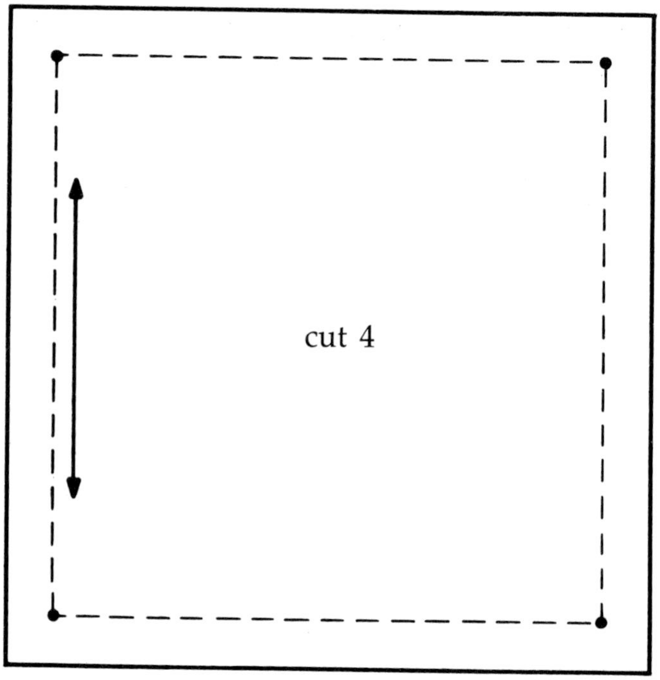

cut 4

Drunkard's Path

10″ square block; intermediate
2 templates; 32 pieces

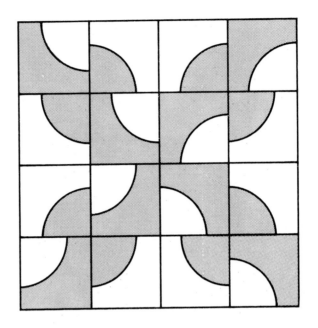

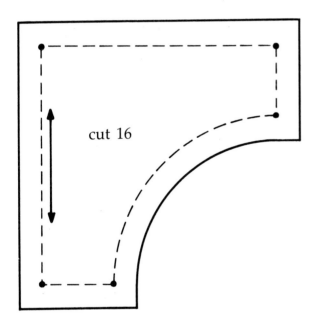

cut 16

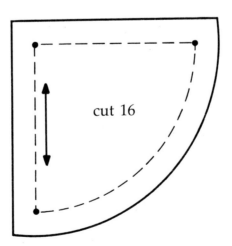

cut 16

Feathered Star

14″ square; advanced
10 templates; 141 pieces

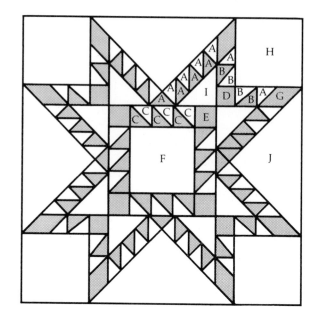

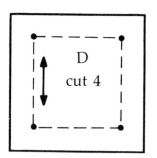

D
cut 4

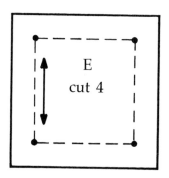

E
cut 4

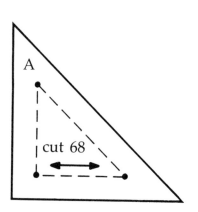

A

cut 68

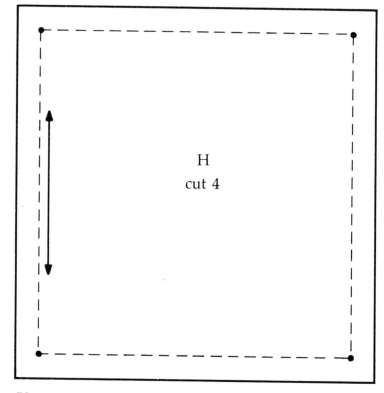

H
cut 4

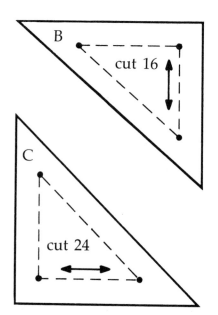

B

cut 16

C

cut 24

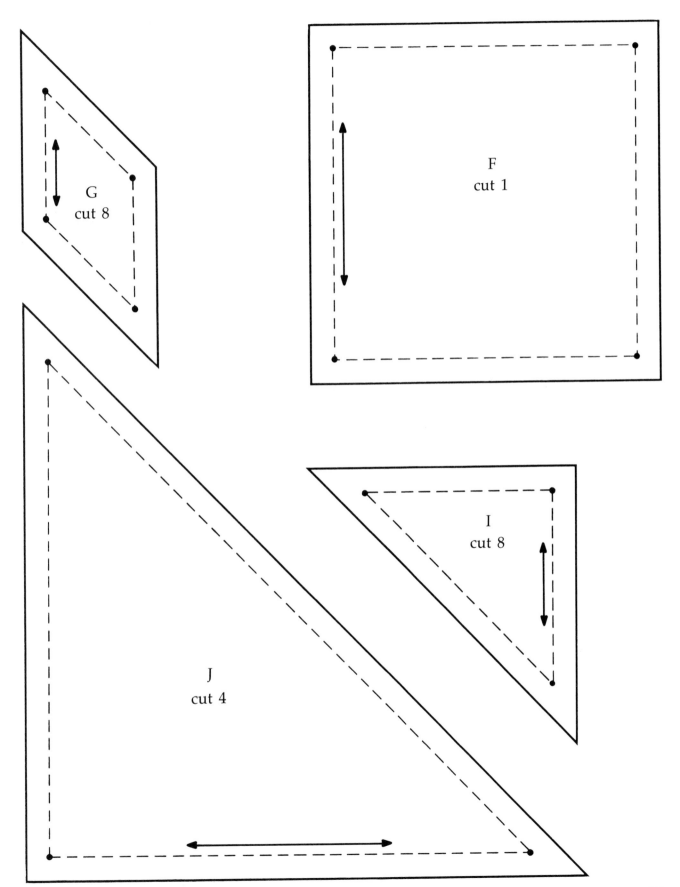

G
cut 8

F
cut 1

I
cut 8

J
cut 4

Square & Star

10" square block; intermediate
5 templates; 37 pieces

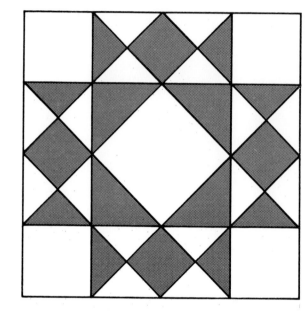

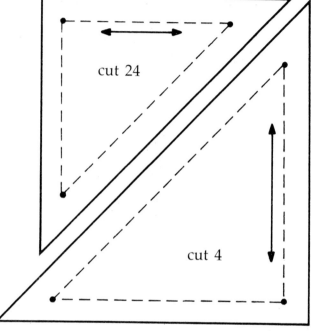

cut 24

cut 4

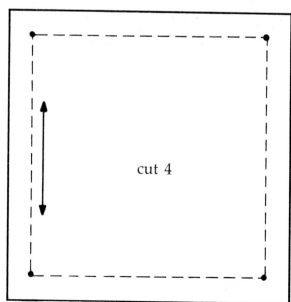

cut 4

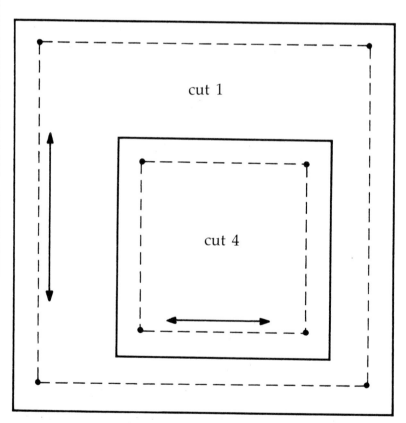

cut 1

cut 4

Ohio Star

10″ square block; intermediate
2 templates; 21 pieces

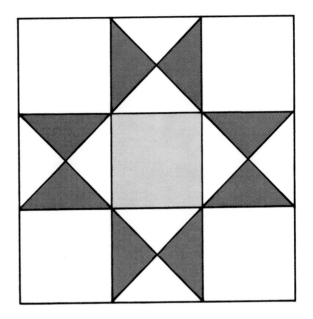

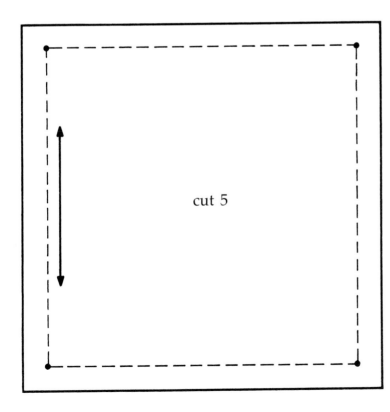

cut 5

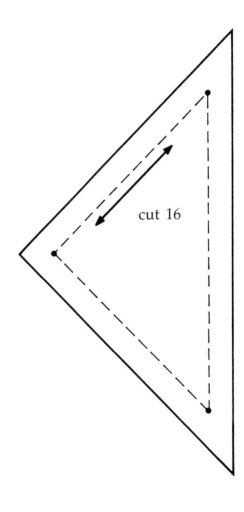

cut 16

Whig Rose

10″ square block; advanced
7 templates; 34 pieces

Use bias tape for stems.
Embroider centers of
small flowers.

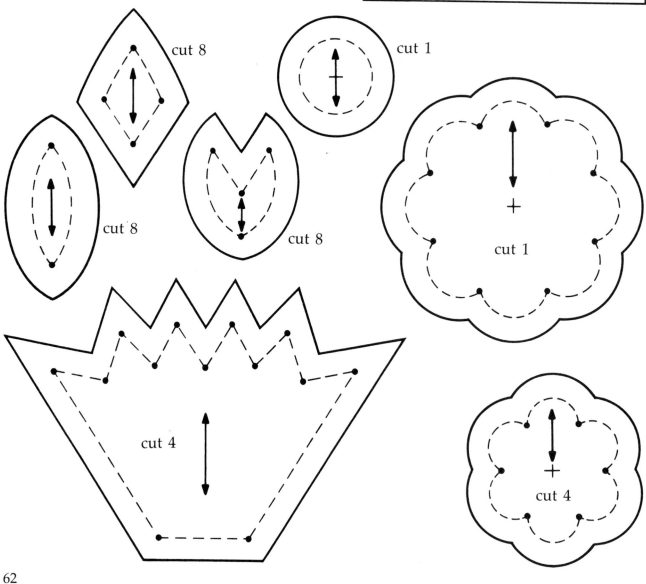

cut 8

cut 1

cut 8

cut 8

cut 1

cut 4

cut 4

Hearts & Gizzards

10" square block; intermediate
2 templates; 12 pieces

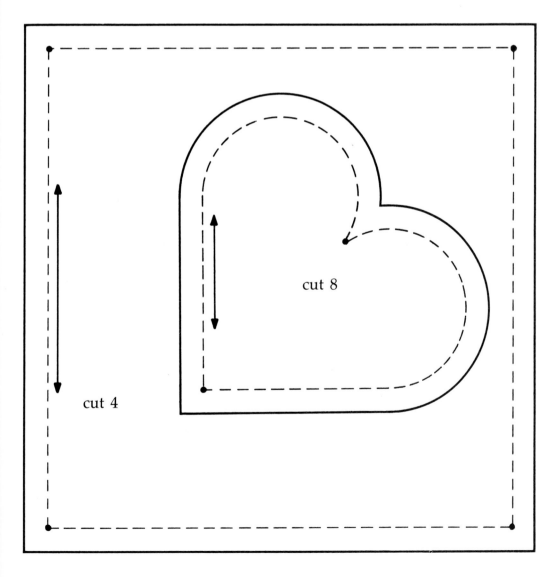

cut 8

cut 4

Hearts

10″ square block; intermediate
4 templates; 5 pieces (including
background square)

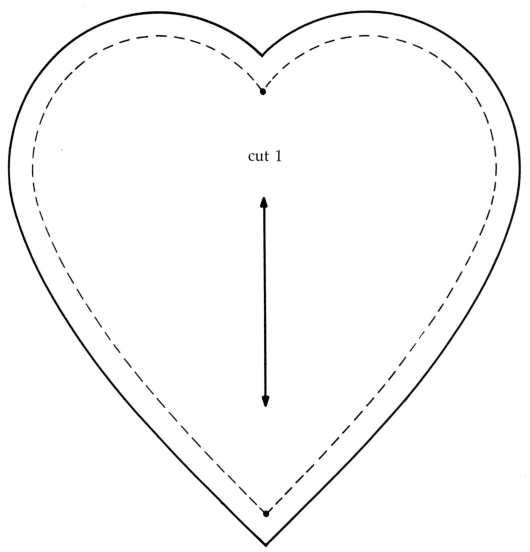

cut 1

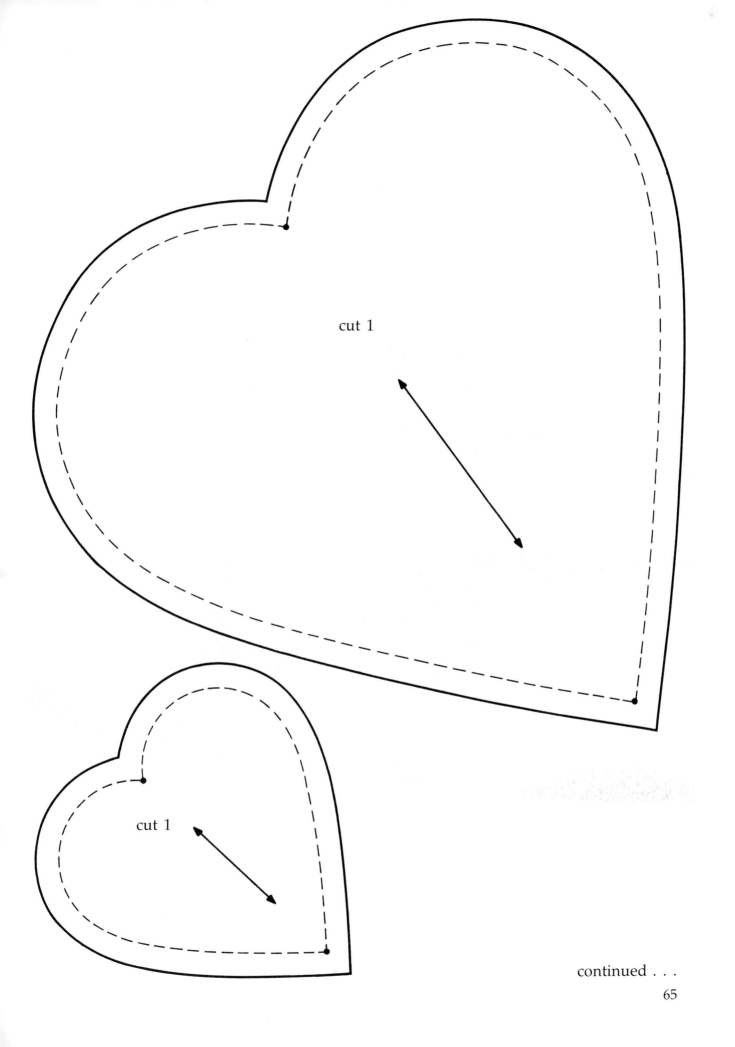

cut 1

cut 1

continued . . .

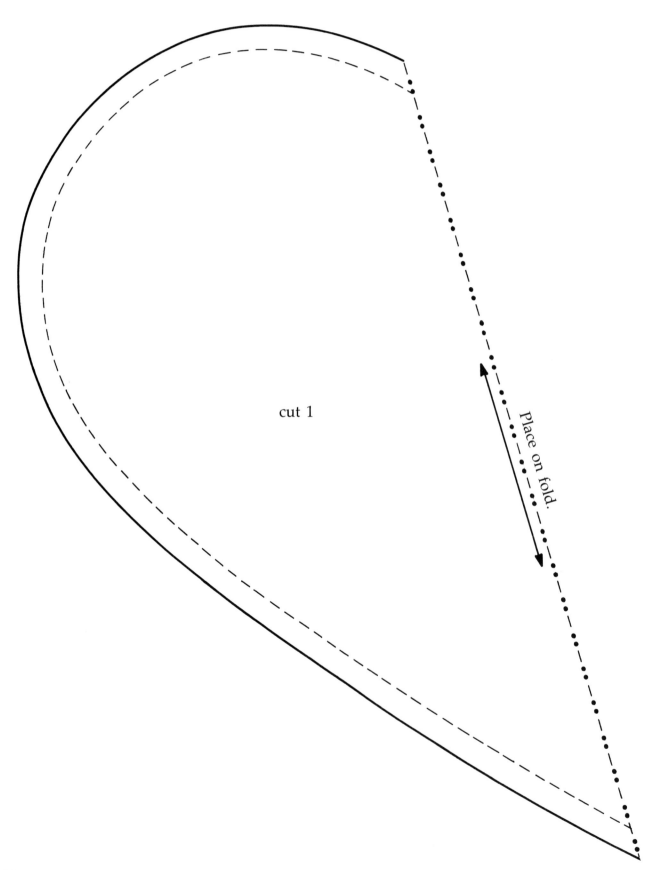

cut 1

Place on fold.

Princess Feather

10″ square block; advanced
2 templates; 10 pieces
(including background square)

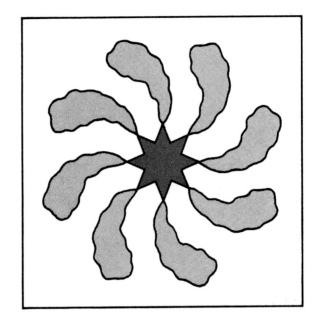

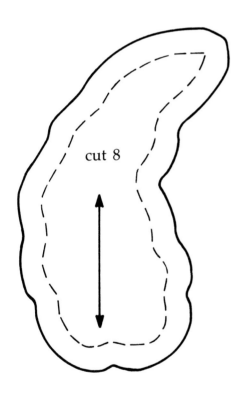

cut 8

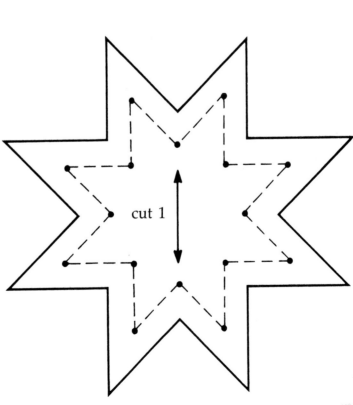

cut 1

Carolina Lily

10″ square block; advanced
8 templates; 31 pieces

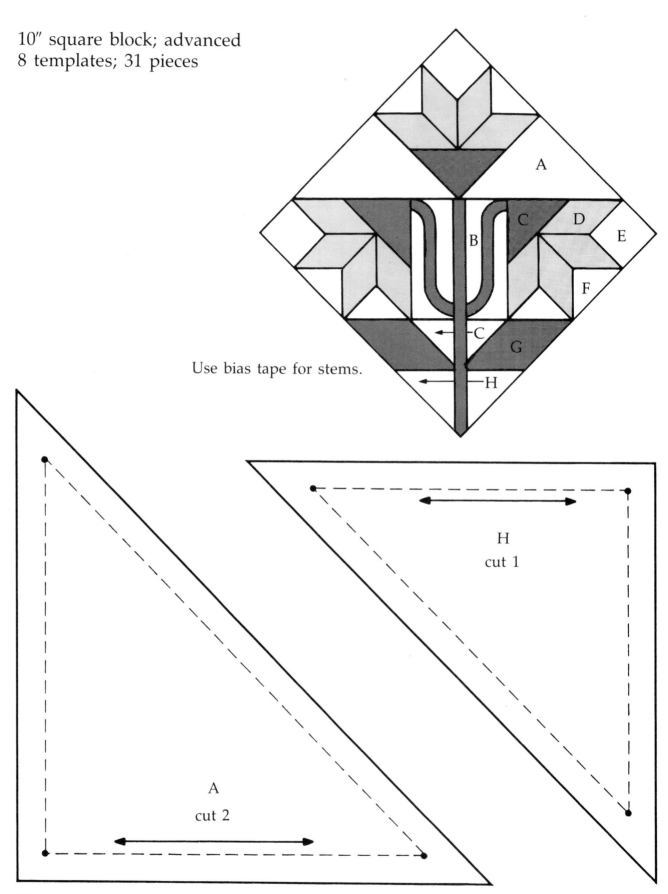

Use bias tape for stems.

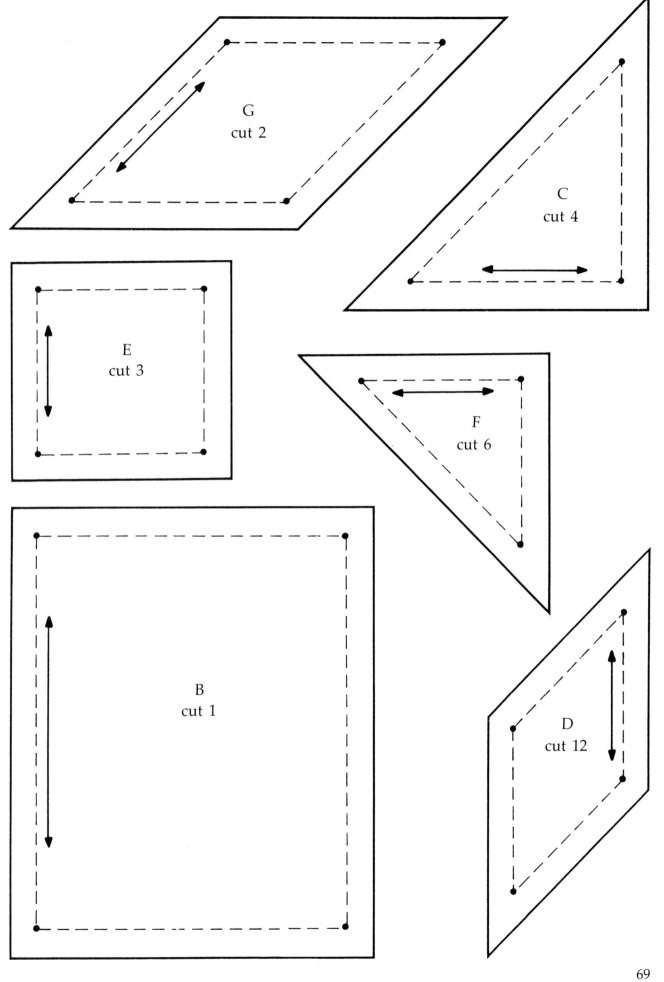

G
cut 2

C
cut 4

E
cut 3

F
cut 6

B
cut 1

D
cut 12

Maple Leaf

10″ square block; beginner
3 templates; 14 pieces

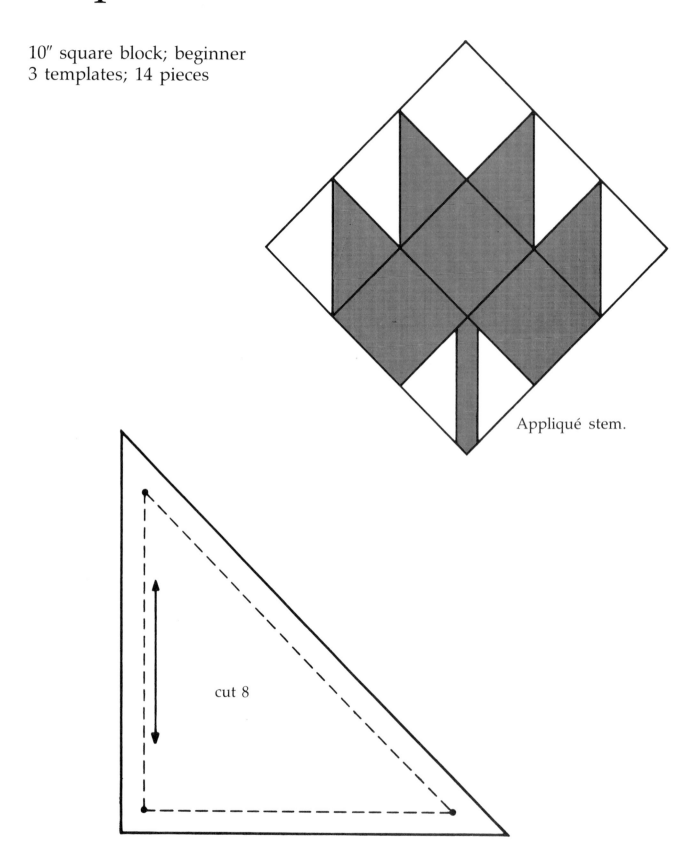

Appliqué stem.

cut 8

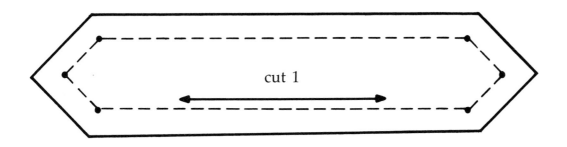

cut 1

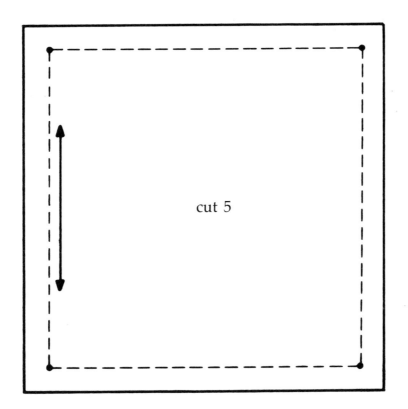

cut 5

Flying Geese

10″ square; intermediate
4 templates; 49 pieces

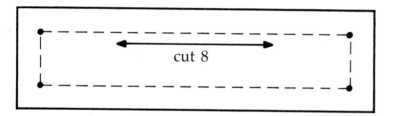

cut 8

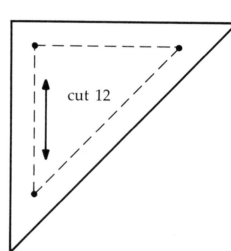

cut 12

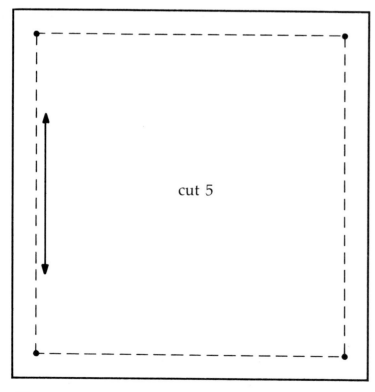

cut 5

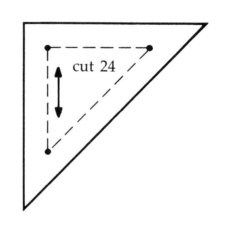

cut 24

Orange Peel

10″ square block; advanced
2 templates, 32 pieces

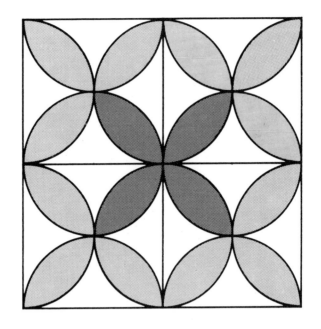

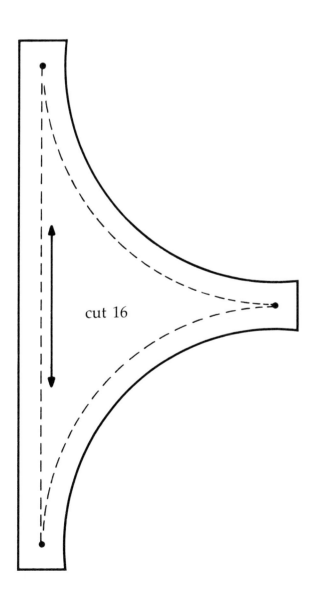

cut 16

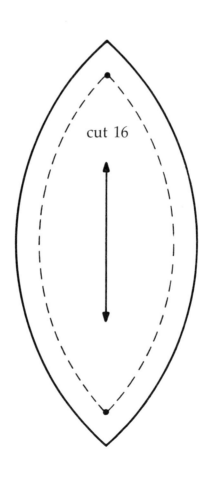

cut 16

Double Wedding Ring

Circle approximately 15″ in
  diameter; advanced
5 templates; 93 pieces

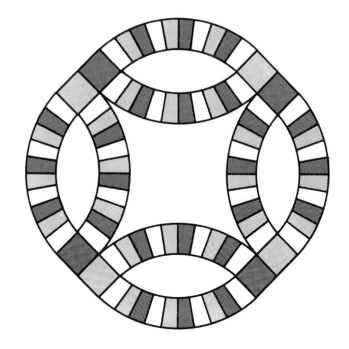

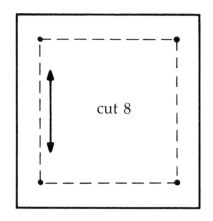

cut 8

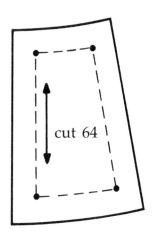

cut 64

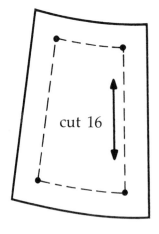

cut 16

Use this piece
to join pieced
strips to
squares.

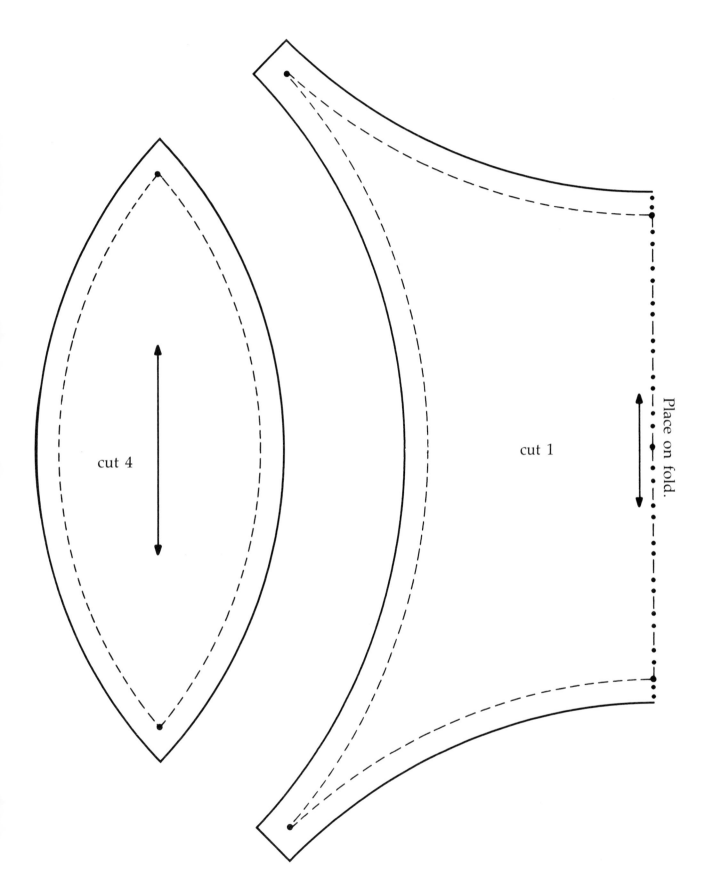

cut 4

cut 1

Place on fold.

Oak Leaf & Swag

10" square block; intermediate
3 templates; 10 pieces
(including background square)

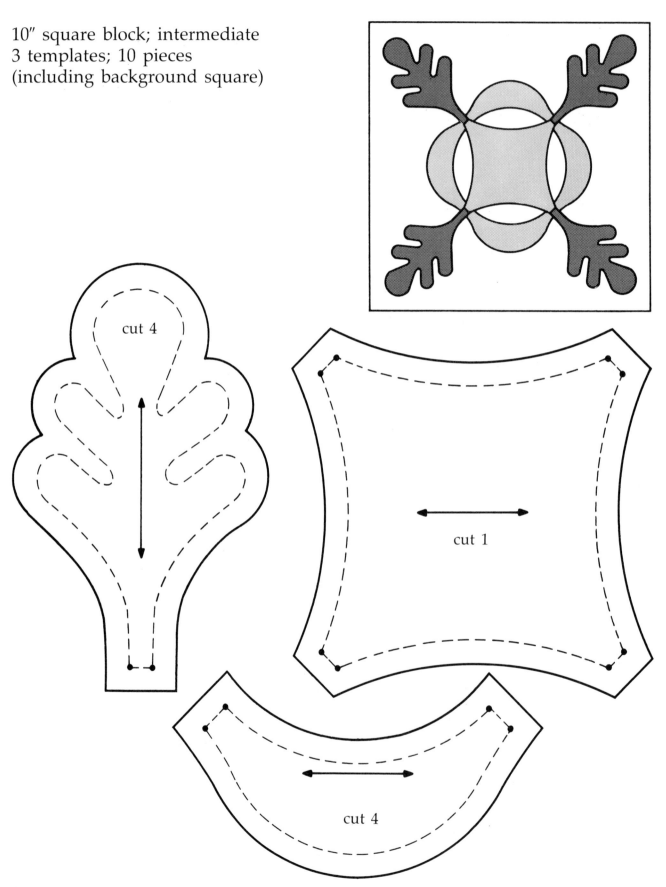

cut 4

cut 1

cut 4

President's Wreath

10″ square block; advanced
3 templates; 21 pieces
(including background square)

Use bias tape for stem.

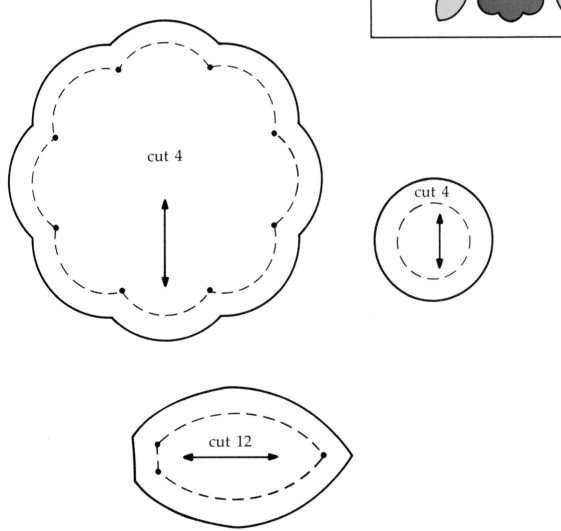

cut 4

cut 4

cut 12

Whig's Defeat

14″ square block; advanced
5 templates; 106 pieces
(including background square)

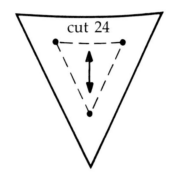

cut 24

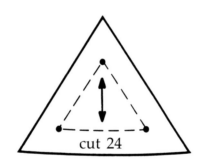

cut 24

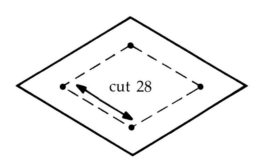

cut 28

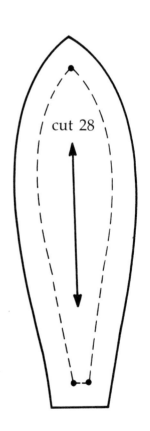

cut 28

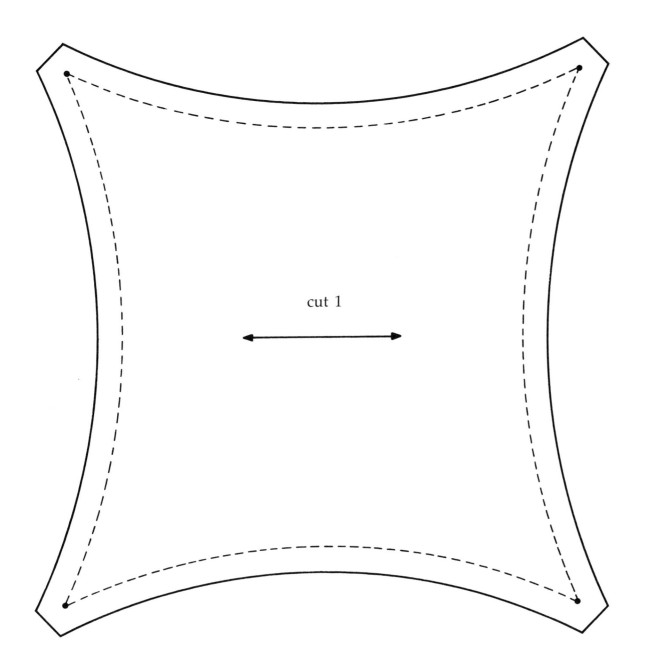

cut 1